The Big Book of Senior Moments

The Big Book of Senior Moments

Humorous Jokes and Anecdotes as a Reminder That We All Forget

Bennett E. Melville

Skyhorse Publishing

Skyhorse Publishing books may be purchased in bulk at special discounts for sales promotion, corporate gifts, fund-raising, or educational purposes. Special editions can also be created to specifications. For details, contact the Special Sales Department, Skyhorse Publishing, 307 West 36th Street, 11th Floor, New York, NY 10018 or info@skyhorsepublishing.com.

Skyhorse® and Skyhorse Publishing® are registered trademarks of Skyhorse Publishing, Inc.®, a Delaware corporation.

Visit our website at www.skyhorsepublishing.com.

10 9 8 7 6 5 4 3

Library of Congress Cataloging-in-Publication Data is available on file.

Cover design by Jane Sheppard

Print ISBN: 978-1-63450-361-7
Ebook ISBN: 978-1-63450-941-1

Printed in China

To my friend Dan, in case he forgot all his help on this.

CONTENTS

INTRODUCTION   viii

CHAPTER ONE: CRIME DOES NOT PAY, BUT BEING A BONEHEAD

MAKES IT MORE INTERESTING   xviii

CHAPTER TWO: FAMOUS FORGETTERS   24

CHAPTER THREE: SPORTS   50

CHAPTER FOUR: SEX: LIFE IS SEXUALLY TRANSMITTED   80

CHAPTER FIVE: AT THE GYM   102

CHAPTER SIX: EPITAPHS AND FUNERALS: THE ULTIMATE

SENIOR MOMENTS   114

CHAPTER SEVEN: POLITICS   126

CHAPTER EIGHT: INSPIRATIONS   146

CHAPTER NINE: GOOD IDEAS GONE BAD   176

CONCLUSION   204

INDEX   210

Introduction

The stereotype is hard to forget, and I say this with no sense of irony intended.

A guy of a certain age shuffles though the neighborhood every day around noon in his plaid Bermuda shorts and his bathrobe, singing "Louie Louie" to himself at high volume. It's a bit off-putting at first, but you get used to it. And you notice he's always got a beatific smile on his face.

"He *suffers* from memory loss," the neighbors whisper.

First, it's important to recognize the guy is smiling. He's happy, if maybe a bit oddly dressed.

I'm with him. I don't suffer from memory loss—and those unfortunate mental burps seem to be happening to me with greater regularity these days. I actually enjoy it. I relish the opportunities forgetting gives me. Mental lapses give me a chance to look at things anew every day. And because I started having senior moments in my twenties, I've had a fresh outlook on life for close to forever.

For years I thought it was musician Carlos Santana who said, "Those who cannot remember the past are condemned to repeat it." I held onto that because

I took it as a positive message. Whether you like Santana's music or not—and I do—the expression made sense to me because the guy is still genuinely rocking nearly fifty years after Woodstock. He's been repeating history year in, year out. Was he thus condemned? I don't think so. He's been enjoying it immensely, I would argue.

During that same period, I thought the opening lines of Steppenwolf's "Born to Be Wild" were, "Kitchen water's running. Head out on the highway." I knew I'd certainly head out if I had a leaky faucet driving me crazy.

But I have learned recently it was Spanish philosopher and essayist George Santayana who commented on forgetting the past and repeating it. And I learned only last year that the opening lines to the Steppenwolf classic were "Get your motor runnin'. Head out on the highway."

Oh.

For me, those were both something close to thirty-year senior moments. That says two things. First, we are all capable of senior moments, no matter how old or young we are. And second, and most important, that it really doesn't matter, because if something makes sense, you need nothing else to move ahead with confidence, even if others think you're a few cards short of a deck. Senior moments arrive un-beckoned at any time to anyone, no matter what age we are.

My advice is to simply roll with them and laugh at them. Embrace them. Surround yourself with friends who inhabit the same planet as you. It's fun.

Laugh and move on.

My older brother had a high school friend who once called him to get our home phone number. He had something important he needed to say, he told my brother over the phone. I once went to pick up a date and rang the doorbell. She wasn't there. I returned a half hour later and did the same thing again. She still wasn't there. I tried once more then I gave up. Later she called. How could you miss our date? she asked. I had the right address but the wrong street. End of romance.

In the past month alone I have:

- Spent close to an hour looking for my glasses when they were resting comfortably on top of my head.
- Poured coffee on my Cheerios.

- Texted a friend to say I had lost my phone, then asked him to call so I could hear the ring and find it.
- Completely blanked on why I had called someone the instant they picked up the phone.
- Told someone a sizzling piece of local gossip then realized she was the person who told me in the first place.
- Forgotten my twenty-year-old niece's name.
- Drove off with a cup of Cumberland Farms coffee on the roof of my car.

I don't beat myself up about all this, though. As the poet Ogden Nash once said, "You are only young once, but you can stay immature indefinitely."

A recent study has shown that while the cliché "laughter is the best medicine" might not be totally true, it certainly does help. Humor just might actually improve memory, the study found, by reducing damage caused by the stress hormone cortisol.

I look at my own shaky memory in a more pedestrian fashion. It allows me to watch reruns and think they are new. It gives me license to tell the same stories repeatedly without embarrassment. I can reread the same book multiple times, and still be surprised by the ending. My friends and acquaintances might come to think of me as a colossal bore, but I'm having the time of my life. As a group of former teammates once had printed on a T-shirt, THE OLDER WE GET, THE BETTER WE WERE.

And that's what matters.

And the nice thing about memory loss is that the chances are we're all going to be afflicted at some point and in some fashion. It's an equal opportunity and democratic affliction. All we have to do is just wait. It will happen, and if you are fortunate enough to be among those who are said to "suffer" from memory loss, consider yourself lucky.

Forgetting makes things real and challenging, and you can have great unexpected excitement without ever leaving home. It makes losing your keys an adventure. It kills time and makes the day go faster. I spent an entire afternoon recently looking for my car keys, which were in the ignition, where I had left them so I would know where they were. I killed a whole evening after dinner a week ago trying to remember the name of the television serious about the French foreign legion starring Buster Crabbe that I enjoyed as a kid. It was *The French Foreign Legion*. I might have drawn the connection earlier, but then what would I have done for the rest of the night?

Today, I can remember the lyrics to songs that were playing thirty years ago, even though I can't remember what I just walked into the kitchen to get.

You will find in these pages what I hope is a celebration of age and forgetting, of brain freezes and mental cramps and senior moments. We've earned them. Here also you will find some inspiration by reading of late-blooming writers like J. R. R. Tolkien and Laura Ingalls Wilder, athletes who went out gracefully and with dignity, ninety-year-old marathoners, and old geezers who conquered Everest. You'll find plenty of people who have managed to live past fifty and have not only enjoyed it, but flourished. Many of today's cultures worship youth. I say that is wrong. Celebrate longevity and all the things that go along with it.

I once worked with a guy years ago who at the advanced age of about thirty basically stopped doing anything physical. He felt he had reached the peak of his vitality. This was based on his cockeyed theory that we all have only a finite number of heartbeats per lifetime. Doing anything that increased those heartbeats was spending money in the bank, he felt. Walking up a flight of stairs would worry him and have him silently counting the extra pumps he had just spent.

He was miserable, an old man at thirty. He was missing the point.

Human life expectancy has increased more in the past fifty years than it did in the previous two hundred thousand years of human existence. In 1950, the average life expectancy was forty-seven; now it is more than seventy.

Think about this: The human brain has an average weight of less than two pounds or so. It looks like a soppy sponge and some days I think mine works like one. But it contains millions of neurons and trillions of synapses that provide an astounding amount of gifts to us all. The brain could be the most complex thing in the entire universe. At a certain age, mine for example, the brain becomes more like an overflowing sieve. It doesn't work right. I say, so what? I know I'm not alone. When I talk to my contemporaries, they're all worrying about the same problems.

So there might be a few missed connections along the way. In middle age, people's brains can start to slow down—a process that it is both terrifying and enlightening. Again, so what? It's not a big deal. Look for the positive side of things. I like enlightenment.

A recent study found that Google has led to memory loss in far more people, younger folks at that, than had been previously thought. Being able to look something up on the Internet has replaced the need and energy to recall a fact. Just grab your phone and the answer is there. Personally I find this a bit of an overreaction, as if we're all going to end up like the legless amoeba-like science fiction people predicted because of the use of automobiles.

I predict that the Internet and Google will have no more to do with memory loss than the legless globular people many thought would be inertly ruling the Earth by now.

You don't need Google. You just need to be patient and wait. It will come.

And you certainly will not be alone, as you will see throughout this book. There's Jimmy Carter forgetting top secret nuclear launch codes in a suit he had sent to the dry cleaners. There's Albert Einstein forgetting where he lived and George W. Bush, the walking Presidential senior moment.

Live well. Be honest. Roll with the punches. Don't take yourself too seriously.

As Mark Twain once said, "If you tell the truth, you don't have to remember anything."

I'll vote for that.

Crime Does Not Pay, but Being a Bonehead Makes It More Interesting

People who need money seem to be overtaken by senior moments more than others, regardless of age. There is just something about the thought of a few quick bucks that puts the brain into idle and keeps it there. Sometimes it's not just the money, though. It also seems that being around law enforcement officials just brings out strong tendencies to do incredibly stupid things.

They'll Be There Soon

When a forty-year-old woman locked herself out of her Pittsburgh home, she sought help from the authorities.

First, she set her house on fire. Then she called 911, expecting the fire department to put out the fire and unlock her door. As planned, the fire department responded, but so did the police, who charged her with reckless endangerment.

Question: How many retirees does it take to change a light bulb?

Answer: Only one, but it might take all day.

Always Count Your Change

A man walked into a Louisiana convenience store, placed a $20 bill on the counter and asked for change. When the clerk opened the cash drawer, the man pulled a gun and asked for all the cash in the register. The clerk immediately complied, and the robber grabbed the cash and rushed out of the store. He left his $20 bill on the counter. Total amount of cash the intrepid robber got away with? $15.

"I always wanted to be somebody. I see now that I should have been more specific."
—Lily Tomlin

Step One: Choose the Right Place to Rob

A Washington state man chose a gun shop for his inaugural armed robbery, beginning the first of series of seriously bad decisions. It would also be his last. The shop was crowded with customers and Washington is a state that allows concealed carrying of firearms. On his way into the shop, the would-be armed robber actually had to step around a police car parked in front, and the officer was inside having coffee with the owner. Our hero walked in, announced a hold up and fired a few wild shots before the police officer, the owner of the shop, and several customers returned fire. They did not miss.

Riding on a Pony

A trail of macaroni salad led police investigators in upstate New York to three suspected burglars.

Deputies near Rochester responded to a burglary at a local restaurant early one morning, after the owners reported their surveillance system and cash register were missing. The investigation led police to a hiking and biking path, where they found cash register parts, surveillance system parts, rubber gloves, loose change and "a steady trail of macaroni salad," according to a news release issued by the office.

"It was later discovered that the suspects stole a large bowl of macaroni salad, which they took turns eating, along their escape route," the statement read.

Nice If It Works

An eighty-six-year-old Japanese woman who allegedly carried on cashing her parents' pension for half a century after they died was arrested recently in Japan.

Mitsue Suzuki is believed to have collected more than 50 million yen over the last five decades for her parents, who both died in the 1960s.

"These days about half the stuff in my shopping cart says, 'For fast relief . . .'"
—Anonymous

Smart Ass

Two young businessmen in Florida were sitting down for a break in their soon-to-be new store in the shopping mall. As yet, the store's merchandise wasn't in—only a few shelves and display racks were set up.

One said to the other, "I'll bet that any minute now some senior is going to walk by, put his face to the window, and ask what we're selling."

Sure enough, just a moment later, a curious senior gentleman walked up to the window, looked around intensely, and rapped on the glass.

Then in a loud voice he asked, "What are you selling here?"

One of the men replied sarcastically, "We're selling ass holes."

Without skipping a beat, the old timer said, "You must be doing well. Only two left."

"I am so old that when I was young the Dead Sea was only sick."
—George Burns

A Billion Here, A Billion There

A Florida man last year walked into the Jacksonville Bank of America and attempted to cash a check for $368,000,000,000.00.

Armed with his identification and fully expecting the check to be cashed, Waters was befuddled when he learned that the blank check that he bought from a homeless man called Tito was unusable.

When the tellers became suspicious, Waters explained that a homeless man by the name of Tito Watts had sold him the blank US Bank of Idaho check (which was issued in the nineties) for $100.

Tito told the man he can go ahead and cash the check for whatever amount his heart desires.

"Tito said the check was good for any amount I wanted to write it for. So blame Tito, not me. I'm as innocent as a schoolgirl," he told tellers.

Not wanting to go small and write a check for a few measly hundreds, thousands or millions—the man had his eyes set on becoming an instant billionaire.

He even planned on opening a one-of-a-kind Italian restaurant with his imaginary billions.

So he made the check out to "cash" and headed to the bank with high hopes.

"It's always been my dream to own the best Italian restaurant on the earth," he later told the police.

But Really . . .

After fifteen months on the lam and with his conscience weighing on him, a Swedish murder suspect decided to turn himself in to police officers. When he arrived at the police station shortly after 6 p.m., cops told him to go away—they were closed for the day. "Closed?" he shouted back at the police. "I'm suspected of murder and am a wanted man. You guys really want to get a hold of me." Obviously not as badly as he'd thought, because officers directed him to colleagues at another police station, who, they assured him, would be happy to arrest him.

"I was taught to respect my elders, but it keeps getting harder to find one."
—Anonymous

Vote Early and Often

During one recent election a casino worker in Las Vegas was irked that people were not taking voter fraud more seriously. So she set out to prove that it was a real problem.

She was caught attempting to vote twice and arrested on charges of voter fraud.

"When you are younger you get blamed for crimes you never committed and when you're older you begin to get credit for virtues you never possessed. It evens itself out."
—Casey Stengel

Gun and Airports

A passenger who tried to bring a loaded gun onto a plane in Chicago had a great excuse. A wonderful try, but it didn't help.

He said he simply forgot he was packing heat.

The man was stopped by security and arrested at Chicago's Midway International Airport when they spotted a .38 caliber revolver, loaded with four live rounds, in the man's bag. Transportation Security Administration (TSA) agents noticed the gun's outline when his bag went through the X-ray machine. The twenty-three-year-old told TSA agents that he forgot the gun was in his bag.

He was arrested and charged with one felony count of boarding an aircraft with a weapon.

"Anyone who has never made a mistake has never tried anything new."
—*Albert Einstein*

Department of Redundancy Department

A twenty-seven-year-old Denver resident doubled his trouble.

After being convicted on theft charges—for stealing a GPS device—the man was fitted with an ankle monitor that allowed the court to track his whereabouts. He didn't let the tracking bracelet stop him from burglarizing fifteen houses while wearing it. While he allegedly made off with some nice hauls—one victim reported that $90,000 worth of goods had been stolen—his glory was short-lived. When he was arrested after one burglary, cops were able to use the GPS data from his ankle bracelet to tie him to the others. He was convicted and sent to another place where police know where he is: prison.

"It is a blessing to get old. It is a blessing to find the time to do the things, to read the books, to listen to the music . . . I have nothing now but praise for my life."
—Maurice Sendak

Question: Among retirees, what is considered formal attire?
Answer: Tied shoes.

"Here is my biggest takeaway after sixty years on the planet: There is great value in being fearless. For too much of my life, I was too afraid, too frightened by it all. That fear is one of my biggest regrets."
—Diane Keaton

"The secret of staying young is to live honestly, eat slowly, and lie about your age."
—Lucille Ball

Wisdom of the Ages

When a grandmother was in her late eighties, she decided to move to Israel.

As part of the preparations, she went to see her doctor and get all her charts. The doctor asked her how she was doing, so she gave him the litany of complaints—this hurts, that's stiff, I'm tired and slower, she reported. The doctor responded with, "Mrs. Siegel, you have to expect things to start deteriorating. After all, who wants to live to 100?"

The grandmother looked him straight in the eye and replied, "Anyone who's 99."

Rule One: Recognize Talent

In an effort to help rehabilitate inmates, a prison in England offered adult education classes to its convicts.

One prisoner used his class time in an IT course to hack the prison's computer system. Why was this man incarcerated in the first place? Oh, yeah, for hacking computers.

"I've been attending lots of seminars in my retirement. They're called naps."
—Merri Brownworth

"I don't feel old. I don't feel anything till noon. That's when it's time for my nap."
—Bob Hope

Rest in Pieces

A New Hampshire woman who told police she dug up her father's grave in search of his "real will" but found only vodka and cigarettes was sentenced recently to one and a half years to three years in prison. She told police last year she dug up the grave "with respect" and her father "would be okay with it."

The fifty-three-year-old was one of four accused in the plan to open her father's vault, then rifle through his casket last in a scheme that a prosecutor compared to an Edgar Allan Poe story. Two pleaded guilty and one was acquitted.

Police said the woman felt she was shorted in her share of the inheritance after her father died in 2004. But no will was found in the casket.

A local paper reported that the judge in the case noted the smashed concrete vault that housed the coffin of Eddie Nash and the disturbed body found the next morning.

"The patrolman said the gravesite of Eddie Nash did not look right," Bornstein said. "That is the understatement of the century."

The remains have since been re-interred at the cemetery.

Second Chance Dummy

A twenty-year-old Chicago resident in court to apply for the city's "second chance program" related to a felony marijuana offense was arrested after court security officers found pot on him.

The young defendant was charged with misdemeanor marijuana possession after officers found 1.4 grams of marijuana in his pocket as he was going through security at the St. Charles courthouse, according to a sheriff's report.

"I forgot I had this in my pocket," he was quoted as telling officers.

Off to a Good Start

A newlywed bride was forced to retrieve her husband's rented tuxedo from the local jail after he was arrested shortly following their wedding ceremony.

Police say the groom was wanted on two domestic relations warrants and two traffic citations. Police were tipped off that the forty-two-year-old was getting married at a church near Allentown, Pennsylvania.

Officers made the arrest shortly after the groom said "I do." The groom was not allowed to stay for his wedding's reception, and his wife had to go to the Carbon County Prison to retrieve his rented tux.

The Perfect Wife

A senior citizen said to his eighty-year-old buddy: "So I hear you're getting married?"

"Yep!"

"Do I know her?"

"Nope!"

"This woman, is she good looking?"

"Not really."

"Is she a good cook?"

"Naw, she can't cook too well."

"Does she have lots of money?"

"Nope! Poor as a church mouse."

"Well, then, is she good in bed?"

"I don't know."

"Why in the world do you want to marry her then?"

"Because she can still drive after dark!"

"Old age is clearly a case of mind over matter. If you don't mind, it doesn't matter."
—Satchel Paige

Leave No Child Behind

Bring Your Child to Work Day is a time-honored tradition that allows children to experience the business world while watching their parents ply their trade. With that in mind, one father brought his young son along with him on a job.

His job happened to be robbing a pet expo. He was caught soon after, in part because of what he'd left behind—his son.

"A man growing old becomes a child again."
—Sophocles

Caregiving Child

"My parents and I were in a doctor's waiting room. We saw an old friend and talked with him and then went back to our seats. Mom (who is deaf) kept saying over and over REALLY loud, 'Wow, has he gained a lot of weight. Looks like he's really going downhill.' I couldn't make her stop, so I just died inside and smiled outside. I tried to say 'sorry' by osmosis to the dear man."

—From a Caregiving Child

"My 83-year-old mother is living with us now. We finally got her to go out and eat one night. We got our food, and she said LOUDLY, 'Well, no wonder you all never lose weight.' I wanted to crawl under the table."
—From a Caregiving Child

"My mother can't hear to follow conversation in a noisy environment, so she just sits quietly and doesn't participate. During a loud family get-together, my oldest son was pondering what he should get his best friend as a wedding gift. Out of the blue, my conservative mom yells loudly, 'CONDOMS!' The room went silent until we all bursting out laughing!"
—From a Caregiving Child

The Duke's Best Day

At high noon on a cold November day in 1974, sixty-seven-year-old John Wayne faced off with the staff of the *Harvard Lampoon* on the famous campus in Cambridge, Massachusetts. The students had issued their challenge by calling the beloved American icon a fraud. Wayne, who had his new movie *McQ* to promote, responded by saying he would be happy to show his film in the pseudo-intellectual swamps of Harvard Square. After the screening, without writers, the former USC footballer delivered a classic performance. When one smart young man asked where he got his phony toupee, Wayne insisted the hair was real. It wasn't his, but it was real. The appreciative underclassmen loved him and after the Q and A session, they all sat down to dinner. Later Wayne, who was suffering greatly from both gout and the after effects of lung cancer (sadly the Duke only had five years to live), said that day at Harvard was the best time he ever had.

A Wise Man, Or Just a Wise Guy

I've sure gotten old! I've had two bypass surgeries, a hip replacement, and new knees. I have fought prostate cancer and diabetes. I'm half blind, can't hear anything quieter than a jet engine, take forty different medications that make me dizzy, winded, and subject to blackouts.

I have bouts with dementia. I have poor circulation; hardly feel my hands and feet anymore. Can't remember if I'm eighty-five or ninety-two. I've lost all my friends. But, thank God, I still have my driver's license.

"Half our life is spent trying to find something to do with the time we have rushed through life trying to save."
—*Will Rogers*

Seemed Like a Good Idea at the Time

A nineteen-year-old man from College Station, Texas, was apparently goofing around with some friends when, somehow, he got his right hand caught in a set of handcuffs. The young man and his friends did not know how to remove them so they decided to visit the local police station to see if the cops might be able to set him free.

This would have been a good idea, if not for two things. First, the young man was wanted on an outstanding warrant for criminal mischief. Second, he had a small amount of marijuana in his front pocket when he walked into the police station.

"For somebody to come in with handcuffs, a warrant, and marijuana. In twenty-seven years this has never happened before," one officer told the local newspaper after booking the young man.

"The older I get the more things I gotta leave behind."
—*Sylvester Stallone as Rocky Balboa*

Check First

Christopher Lowcock was under house arrest in England on drug and weapons charges. To make sure he would not violate curfew, police attached an electronic tag to his leg. The problems for police started when the leg they attached the tag to was prosthetic. Lowcock simply took it off and headed out for a well-deserved night on the town.

"The difference between genius and stupidity is that genius has its limits."
—*Albert Einstein*

Brotherly Love

A Pittsburgh man charged with attacking his brother with a baseball bat made bail, promising to return to court when his trial came around. But when that day came he was nowhere in sight, an absence that landed him on the Allegheny County Top 20 Most Wanted Fugitives List.

If this story ended there it might have been merely interesting. What made it even more so was his later arrest. Shortly after his successful election, Pittsburgh Mayor-elect Bill Peduto hosted a victory party at the greater Pittsburgh Coliseum, featuring free food, free beer, and lots and lots of concerned citizens. One of those citizens noticed that one of the Peduto supporters lounging around the beverage table looked a lot like the noted bail jumper.

He was arrested by another party attendee, a Pittsburgh cop.

Question: When is a retiree's bedtime?
Answer: Three hours after he falls asleep on the couch.

"As men get older, the toys get more expensive."
—*Marvin Davis*

"No man is ever old enough to know better."
—*Holbrook Jackson*

Famous Forgetters

The culture of narcissism, of loving oneself and spending long hours being uncomfortable without a mirror nearby, has long bred an amazing and rich mine at which others can find mother lodes of dumbness. Maybe it's related to too much time in the spotlight. All those glaring cameras and uninterrupted attention makes it hard to think clearly.

> *"Inside every old person is a young person wondering what happened."*
> —Terry Pratchett

Check the Pockets

Jimmy Carter once left the uber-secret codes for emergency nuclear launches in his suit coat and sent it to the dry cleaners.

> *"All of us could take a lesson from the weather. It pays no attention to criticism."*
> —Anonymous

The First Famous Forgetter?

Ansel Bourne was a well-known evangelical preacher from Greene, Rhode Island, who took a trip to visit his sister in Providence on January 17, 1887. For unexplained reasons, he ended up withdrawing his savings instead and traveling to Norristown, Pennsylvania. While there, he decided to open up a variety store under the name Albert J. Brown and started a new life.

When Bourne woke up on the morning of March 15, he had no idea where he was. He became very confused when residents told him his name was Albert J. Brown. In his mind, it was still January 17 and he had no memory of his previous two months in Norristown. After returning to Rhode Island, Bourne was studied by the Society for Physical Research. Under hypnosis, he would assume the persona of Albert J. Brown. The hypnotized Bourne told a back story about Brown that was similar to his own, but denied knowledge of anyone named Ansel Bourne. It was probably the first documented case of a psychiatric disorder known as the "fugue state," a form of amnesia that causes a person to lose their identity for a period of time before their memory suddenly returns. After the hypnosis, Ansel Bourne lived out the rest of his life without incident and never assumed the persona of Albert J. Brown again.

"Isn't it funny how day by day nothing changes, but when we look back everything is different."
—C. S. Lewis
"A clear conscience is usually the sign of a bad memory."
—Stephen Wright

White House Forgetter

Raymond Robins was a noted economist and advocate of organized labor who often worked closely with the White House on such issues as prohibition and establishing diplomatic relations with Russia. On September 3, 1932, Robins had a meeting scheduled with President Herbert Hoover, but never showed up. He was last seen leaving the City Club in Manhattan. Robins's disappearance made headlines, leading to speculation that he might have been the victim of organized crime, but there were also reported sightings of him acting strangely while wandering the streets of Chicago. On November 18, Robins was discovered living under the name Reynolds H. Rogers in Whittier, a small town in the mountains of North Carolina.

Robins had apparently arrived in the town one week after he disappeared, claiming that he was a miner from Kentucky. He lived in a boarding house, spent most of his time prospecting, and became a popular figure in the community. Even though Robins had a grown a beard by that time, someone recognized him from a photograph in the newspaper and contacted the authorities. Robins' nephew went to Whittier to identify him, but Robins did not recognize him and had no memory of his previous life. After reuniting with his wife and undergoing psychiatric treatment, Robins finally started to regain his memory. It was speculated that a combination of stress and emotional strain might have caused Robins to enter a fugue state, prompting him to assume a new identity.

"Every morning is the dawn of a new error."
—*Anonymous*

Speed the Prompter

Actress Lindsay Lohan made her West End London stage debut, starring in David Mamet's Hollywood satire, *Speed-the-Plow*, and forgot her lines during the second act, even with prompting. One critic was sympathetic, writing "the pressure must have been immense." Other critics were not so kind.

"Lindsay Lohan's acting is that of a not specially gifted schoolgirl," sniffed one.

Where Is Jack?

Actor Jack Nicholson has reportedly retired from acting because his memory will no longer allow him to learn the lines.

> *"Live every day as if it were your last.*
> *Because one day, you'll be right."*
> *—Anonymous*
> *"It's hard to be nostalgic when you can't*
> *remember anything."*
> *—Anonymous*

Oh Say What?

Botched lyrics and technical difficulties made it tough for *American Idol* winner Scotty McCreery to get through the national anthem when he performed it at a World Series game.

First, the country singer had to start the song over after the microphone malfunctioned. Then on his second attempt, he accidentally sang "no Jose" instead of "oh say."

"Now, as I move through my fifties, I can be professional and domestic, creative and intellectual, patient and urgent. I have learned that we should never settle for someone else's definition of who we can be. Growing to this age, I realize, is kind of like feeling your voice deepen. It's still your voice, but it has more substance, and it sounds like it knows its own origins."
—Susan Sarandon

Just Want to Remember

"Girls Just Wanna Have Fun" singer Cyndi Lauper fudged the lyrics to the national anthem while performing at the US Tennis Open in Flushing, New York. Instead of singing, "were so gallantly streaming," the eighties rocker sort of blurted out, "as our flag was still streaming."

It Could Happen to Anyone

The Voice judge Christina Aguilera "got lost in the moment of the song" during her Super Bowl performance recently.

Singing "The Star-Spangled Banner" to kick off the championship game between the Green Bay Packers and the Pittsburgh Steelers, Aguilera messed up the line, "O'er the ramparts we watched, were so gallantly streaming," repeating an earlier line of the song that she also botched.

Aguilera sang "What so proudly we watched at the twilight's last gleaming" instead of the correct lyric, which begins "What so proudly we hailed."

The Great Gambon

The theater world in Britain was shocked after one of its favorite sons, actor Michael Gambon, announced that he would give up live theater work due to failing memory. He would be restricting himself to films and television, areas of the business in which an inability to remember lines is not so cruelly exposed.

Long before he achieved international fame as Professor Dumbledore in the Harry Potter films, "the great Gambon" (as he's universally known within the business) was considered a prodigious talent.

No Place Like Home

Isaac Newton was notorious for forgetting things or getting lost in his own building.

Careful of the First Step

World-renowned mathematician Witold Hurewicz was noted for work in topology and also for being distracted. In 1956 while attending the International Symposium on Algebraic Topology in Uxmal, Mexico, he climbed to the top of a Mayan ziggurat, then forgot where he was. He stepped from the top and fell off to his death—a rather extreme penalty for absentmindedness.

And Don't Come Back

As many of us seniors know, we Silver Surfers know, sometimes we have trouble with our computers.

Yesterday, I had a problem, so I called Georgie, the eleven-year-old year old next door, whose bedroom looks like Mission Control, and asked him to come over.

Georgie clicked a couple of buttons and solved the problem.

As he was walking away, I called after him, 'So, what was wrong?'

He replied, 'It was an ID ten Terror.'

I didn't want to appear stupid but nonetheless inquired, 'An ID ten Terror? What's that? In case I need to fix it again.'

Georgie grinned. 'Haven't you ever heard of an ID ten Terror before?'

'No,' I replied.

'Write it down,' he said, 'and I think you'll figure it out.'

So I wrote down:

ID10T

I used to like the little bastard.

A Relatively Close Call

Albert Einstein used to walk to work at the Institute for Advanced Study in Princeton, New Jersey. Fellow scientist Marston Morse, also at the Institute, drove. Einstein was apparently as distracted a walker as Morse was a driver. While backing out of his driveway, Morse very nearly backed right over the walking Einstein. Fortunately it was only a near miss.

"I may be a senior, but so what? I'm still hot."
—Betty White

Maybe You *Can* Take It with You

Johnson was a man who had worked all of his life, had saved all of his money, and was a real miser when it came to his spending. He told his wife, Marie, "When I die, I want you to take all my money and put it in the casket with me. I want to take my money to the afterlife with me." She promised him with all of her heart that when he died, she would put all of the money in the casket with him.

He died. He was stretched out in the casket. Marie was sitting there in black, and her friend Susan was sitting next to her.

When they finished the ceremony, just before the undertakers got ready to close the casket, Marie said, "Wait just a minute!"

She had a box with her and came over with the box and put it in the casket. Then the undertakers locked the casket down, and they rolled it away.

So Susan said to her, "Marie, I know you weren't fool enough to put all that money in there with your husband."

The always loyal Marie replied, "Listen, I'm a Christian, I can't go back on my word. I promised him that I was going to put that money in that casket with him."

"You mean to tell me you put all that money in the casket with him!?"

"I sure did," said the wife. "I got it all together, put it into my account and wrote him a check. If he can cash it, he can spend it."

"I'm gonna hang a Batman outfit in my closet just to screw with myself when I get Alzheimer's."
—Will Ferrell

Thank God for the Kids

Academy Award winner Angelina Jolie said that her ten-year-old son baked a cake on the day of her wedding to Brad Pitt. The couple also forgot a few other minor parts of the ceremony, like the music and their vows, a London newspaper reported. The actress said that they had a plan for everyone to sing "Here Comes the Bride" beforehand but forgot about it and moved into the ceremony. But they had also forgotten to write vows. The kids again stepped in and wrote them.

"Minds ripen at very different ages."
—Stevie Wonder

She Wasn't Afraid

Virginia Woolf accidentally baked her wedding ring into a pudding.

Need That Thing to Function

Anyone can relate. You get in your car—in this case your helicopter—and you realize you forgot something: glasses, wallet, and cell phone.

So it went for President Barack Obama recently. On his way to Las Vegas for a speech, Obama boarded his Marine One helicopter on the White House's South Lawn.

But he promptly disembarked and headed back into the executive mansion.

When he emerged moments later, the president said he had forgotten his Blackberry, pulling it from its holster and showing it to reporters and photographers.

He's Just My Husband

When actress Hilary Swank won the Best Actress Oscar in 2000 for *Boys Don't Cry*, she forgot to mention then-husband Chad Lowe. She made a point of effusively thanking him in 2005 when she won again for *Million Dollar Baby*.

"I'm going to start by thanking my husband, because I'd like to think I learn from past mistakes," she said.

A General Never Forgets

While the Spanish-American War was some thirty-three years out from the Civil War, there were still officers in the Army who had fought on either side in the Civil War. Major General Joseph Wheeler was one such officer. He saw extensive service in the Civil War as an officer in the Confederate States Army rising from Second Lieutenant to Lieutenant General. He was wounded three times and had a total of sixteen horses shot from under him. He returned home to Alabama as a planter after the war and held a number of elected positions over the years. When the Spanish American

War came up, at sixty-one years old, he volunteered to serve.

As the Rough Riders pushed from their landing place towards their goal of Santiago, their first engagement with the Spanish Army was at Las Guasimas. After a hot engagement, the Spanish soldiers finally broke and retreated toward Santiago.

Major Beach, standing next to Joe Wheeler, watched the departure and Wheeler, forgetting in the heat of the moment which war he was fighting, said, "We've got the damn Yankees on the run!"

"The only source of knowledge is experience."
—*Albert Einstein*

Great Minds Think . . . Differently

Being one of the most important great minds of his century, Albert Einstein was known to suffer from dyslexia, mainly because of his bad memory and his constant failure to memorize the simplest of things. He would not remember the months in the year yet he would succeed in solving some of the most complicated mathematical formulas of the time without any trouble. He may have never learned how to properly tie his shoelaces but his scientific contributions and theories still have a major effect on all of today's current knowledge of science.

It Wasn't Even Thanksgiving

Ben Franklin nearly killed himself giving an electric shock to a turkey.

> *"Some people die at 25 and aren't buried until 75."*
> *—Benjamin Franklin*

A Mystery

Agatha Christie was the most famous mystery writer of all time, so it's only appropriate that she became the center of her own bizarre mystery in 1926. On the evening of December 3, the thirty-six-year-old Christie mysteriously vanished from her home in Sunningdale, England. The next morning, her abandoned car was discovered one hour away in Newlands Corner, but she was nowhere around.

Christie's disappearance became a huge story and once word spread that her husband, Archibald, had recently asked for a divorce, speculation ran rampant that he'd murdered her. Finally, on December 14, Christie was found alive and well, registered under the name Teresa Neele at the Swan Hydropathic Hotel in Harrogate. She claimed to have no memory of how she'd ended up there.

There has always been debate over what happened to Christie during those eleven days. At the time, many believed she staged her own disappearance for publicity or as a way of getting back at her husband— especially since Teresa Neele happened to be the name of his mistress. However, there is evidence that Christie might have entered a fugue state and truly lost her memory.

It has been theorized that Christie's impending divorce and the recent death of her mother caused her to enter a deep depression. Crashing her car might have been the breaking point that caused her to develop amnesia and forget who she was. She died in 1976, and took the full truth about what happened to her grave.

He Could Spell Poem, Though

W. B. Yeats was denied a post at Trinity College in Dublin for spelling "professor" wrong on the application.

Who?

Charles Darwin ate an owl.

Ouch

Edgar Allan Poe split his pants playing leapfrog with his wife.

High Standards

When Fred Astaire was sixty-nine, he gave up dancing, explaining: "At my age, I don't want to disappoint anyone, including myself."

How Philosophical

Gertrude Stein wrote on her philosophy exam, "I am so sorry but I do not feel a bit like an examination in philosophy."

What's to Say?

Isaac Newton served in Parliament for a full year and only spoke one sentence.

"Of all sad words of mouth or pen, the saddest are these: it might have been."
—John Greenleaf Whittier

Oops

Thomas Edison electrocuted an elephant.

Rules of the Road

Mildred was riding in Susan's car to a meeting at the church, and she became increasingly uneasy. "Susie," she said hesitantly, "I don't want to criticize, but you've run two red lights and made an illegal left turn."

"Oh, shit," said Susan. "Am I driving?"

"Don't worry about old age; it doesn't last that long."
—Mark Twain

Senior Challenges

As a senior citizen was driving down the freeway, his car phone rang. Answering, he heard his wife's voice urgently warning him, "Herman, I just head on the news that there's a car going the wrong way on 280. Please be careful!"

"Hell," said Herman. "It's not just one car. It's hundreds of them!"

And for Dessert . . .

Once Beethoven dropped in to a restaurant to have dinner, but because he was very absent-minded he forgot what he actually came there for. He was asked by a waiter a few times what he would like to order but he didn't pay any attention to that. After an hour Beethoven called the waiter and asked him:

"How much do I pay?"

"Sir, you haven't ordered anything yet and I would like to ask you what I can do for you?"

"Just bring whatever you want and leave me alone."

Oh Yeah, And . . .

When Julia Roberts won the Best Actress Oscar for *Erin Brockovich*, she thanked "everyone I have ever met in my life."

Except, apparently the main reason for the film, Erin Brockovich herself, whom she neglected to mention.

She made up for it later at a press conference but it was too late.

Notes Help

The award for most scatterbrained celebrity has to go to former Spice Girl Geri Halliwell, who was once spotted leaving a Post-it note on her dashboard to remind herself to lock the car doors.

Paparazzi photographed the singer while out shopping but one eagle-eyed snapper noticed she had left herself a little reminder plastered to her sat-nav system.

The bright pink note read "Lock Door!" and it seems to have worked but Geri failed to realize the large sat-nav it was stuck to posed a rather intriguing prospect for any thief in the area.

It wasn't the first time Geri has struggled with the basics of driving. Once she turned to ask her followers if it was illegal to tweet while stationary at a red light.

Old Friends

Two elderly ladies had been friends for many decades. Over the years, they had shared all kinds of activities and adventures.

Lately, their activities had been limited to meeting a few times a week to play cards.

One day, they were playing cards when one looked at the other and said,

"Now don't get mad at me.

I know we've been friends for a long time, but I just can't think of your name!

I've thought and thought, but I can't remember it.

Please tell me what your name is."

Her friend glared at her. For at least three minutes she just stared and glared at her.

Finally she said, "How soon do you need to know?"

What's in a Name?

Actress Zoe Saldana keeps forgetting her husband's name. The *Book of Life* actress once claimed that her pregnancy has made her very absent-minded, comparing herself with the famously forgetful fish Dory from *Finding Nemo*. She said: "You forget a lot of things! My husband's name is Marco, and there have been a couple of times I've called him Michael. I have like a Dory brain from *Nemo*—I reset like every three seconds."

"I truly believe that age—if you're healthy—age is just a number."
—*Hugh Hefner*

Where Is That Apple Again?

Isaac Newton was notorious for forgetting things or getting lost in his own building.

Have to Start Somewhere

My young grandson called the other day to wish me Happy Birthday. He asked me how old I was, and I told him, sixty-two. My grandson was quiet for a moment, and then he asked, "Did you start at one?"

Grandparent Wisdom

I was out walking with my four-year-old granddaughter. She picked up something off the ground and started to put it in her mouth. I took the item away from her and I asked her not to do that.

"Why?" my granddaughter asked.

"Because it's been on the ground. You don't know where it's been, it's dirty, and probably has germs," I replied.

At this point, my granddaughter looked at me with total admiration and asked, "Grandma, how do you know all this stuff? You are so smart."

I was thinking quickly, "All Grandmas know this stuff. It's on the Grandma Test. You have to know it, or they don't let you be a Grandma."

We walked along in silence for two or three minutes, but she was evidently pondering this new information.

"Oh . . . I get it!" she beamed, "So if you don't pass the test, you have to be the Grandpa."

"Exactly," I replied.

Sports

Tense and strenuous and exhausting sports have long been a breeding ground for increasing the density inside the heads of athletes. It seems that playing games is the perfect antidote to boredom, common sense, and sharp clear thinking.

"It ain't over till it's over."
—Yogi Berra

"I can't really remember the names of the clubs that we went to."
—Shaquille O'Neal, on whether he had visited the Parthenon during his visit to Greece

"When my time on Earth is gone, and my activities here are past, I want them to bury me upside down, and my critics can kiss my ass."
—Bobby Knight

Waited a Bit Too Long

To show appreciation for their long-suffering fan base in 2006, the lowly Houston Astros invited supporters to come to their ballpark early one day to mingle with former team stars Jose Cruz and Joe Niekro. Joe Niekro was unable to attend due to a death in the family, his own.

"When a man retires, his wife gets twice the husband but only half the income."
—*Chi Chi Rodriguez*

Going Out on Top—While They Could Still Remember

While most athletes cling to the sport they love until they simply can't hold on any longer, in some rare instances sports stars have called it quits while still in the midst of their prime years.

Rocky Marciano retired from boxing at thirty-one before ever tasting defeat, sporting a perfect 49–0 record.

Sandy Koufax shocked the baseball world when he retired at the age of thirty, while he was still the best pitcher on the planet.

Barry Sanders at thirty-one and Michael Jordan at thirty (the first time) retired prematurely when they were still putting their best feet forward.

"The trick is growing up without growing old."
—*Casey Stengel*

Makes Sense

A good-looking and well-preserved woman of about seventy was sitting in a restaurant, eating alone, when an extremely handsome and sexy man of middle years came in and also sat alone. He noticed her staring and, after about half an hour, sent a waiter to her table with this penned message: "If you will tell me—in three words—what you want, I'll follow you home and do it for only $20."

After a moment's deep thought, the woman flipped the note over and wrote, "Clean my house."

"If you don't know where you are going, you might wind up someplace else."
—*Yogi Berra*

Try the Other Direction

The Houston Astros had a horrendous season in 2013, but it was also entertaining. They accidently hit their own teammates, tried out new and unsuccessful bunting techniques, and recreated Jets quarterback Mark Sanchez's famous butt fumble. The Astros continued to impress all year with their unimpressive plays, game after game.

The nightmare of a season is coming to a close for Houston, but that hasn't stopped them from making even more embarrassing plays. During the sixth inning of one of the last games of the season against the Yankees, catcher Matt Pagnozzi attempted to keep tabs on Robinson Cano on the basepaths. Pagnozzi tried to throw down to second base to catch Cano after he took a big lead, but his throw backfired—literally—as he ended up spiking the ball, somehow, and it ended up traveling to the backstop. Lyle Overbay was on third base during the shenanigans, and was able to score on the bizarre throwing error.

"Drink Coffee: Do dumb things faster and with more energy."
—*Anonymous*

Head-Butt Turns into Real Pain in the Neck

In 1997, the Washington Redskins finally made a change at quarterback with Jeff Hostetler replacing Gus Frerotte after one of the more bizarre plays in the team's history. Frerotte did not start the second half of the Redskins' overtime tie against the New York Giants after head-butting a padded wall in the end zone in celebration of a one-yard touchdown run. He ended up with a sprained neck and a trip to the hospital.

On a third-and-goal play from the 1, he had rolled out of the pocket looking for a receiver. When he saw a clear path in front of him, Frerotte dashed toward the goal line and just managed to get into the right front pylon of the south end zone ahead of two Giants defenders.

Frerotte kept running toward the corner of the stadium. First he spiked the football against the wall, then he stopped momentarily and continued celebrating his team's first score by butting the top of his helmeted head into a padded wall. He clearly recoiled after the impact.

As Frerotte trotted back toward the bench area, he winced as he tried to get his helmet off. Several trainers and a team doctor also saw his discomfort, and worked on him as he sat on the Redskins bench during the Giants' next possession.

At halftime, Frerotte underwent X-rays in a facility underneath the stadium. A team spokesman said the X-rays were negative. As a precaution, Frerotte was taken to Prince George's County Hospital by ambulance, accompanied by an unidentified team doctor, during the third quarter.

He was given a CAT scan, the results of which were negative. Frerotte left the hospital midway through the fourth quarter wearing a neck brace. "I feel all right," he said, but declined further comment.

"I went to the doctor today with severe headaches.
He asked me if I'd suffered any memory loss.
How would I know?"
—*Anonymous*

"The worst thing is short term memory loss . . . the worst
thing is short term memory loss . . .
—*Larry King*

Follow the Rules

Hospital regulations require a wheelchair for patients being discharged. However, while working as a student nurse, I found one elderly gentleman already dressed and sitting on the bed with a suitcase at his feet who insisted he didn't need my help to leave the hospital. After a chat about rules being rules, he reluctantly let me wheel him to the elevator. On the way down I asked him if his wife was meeting him. "I don't know," he said. "She's still upstairs in the bathroom changing out of her hospital gown."

Eyes of Texas

Rather than dribble the ball up the floor to try and give himself a better chance at burying a game-winner, former Texas Longhorn Roscoe Smith heaved a shot from about three-quarters length—with nearly ten seconds left in the half. He did it again in the second half. Too many energy drinks at halftime?

"I keep myself right at the (professional) level, in case somebody feels froggy and says, 'I think I'm going to whup the old man,'" he says. "And they'd be shocked."
—Evander Holyfield

The Moroccan Flash

While international soccer fans adore Ronaldinho for his bright personality and on-field flare, Khalid Askri is giving the Brazilian playmaker a run for his money in Morocco.

Askri's clutch saves in an extra-time quarterfinal victory over Mexican club Monterrey helped Raja advance to the semi-finals, where the Moroccan team will face the Copa Libertadores winners.

For a player dubbed "the unluckiest goalkeeper in the world," Askri gave Raja chance of becoming the first African team to reach the 2014 Club World Cup final.

Askri earned the title in September 2010 when a pair of mistakes cost his then club FAR Rabat. First, celebrating a penalty save, he tossed the ball, only to have backspin carry the ball into goal to his shock. He followed that up weeks later with an embarrassing giveaway that led to a goal. After which he ripped off his shirt and stormed off the field despite pleas from his teammates to continue.

"I owe a lot to my parents, especially my mother and father."
—Greg Norman

Nice Block(head)

An unusual lock in a game between powerhouse Florida and underling Georgia Southern some much-needed comic relief.

"I thought it was comical," senior offensive guard Jon Halapio said after the game.

"We were all in the locker room joking around about it."

On the first play of the second half and senior wide receiver Solomon Patton took a jet sweep off right tackle. Senior center Jonotthan Harrison pulled and got locked up with junior wide receiver Quinton Dunbar. The two Gators remained engaged throughout the play, seemingly unaware of each other's orange-and-blue uniforms.

"Perfect technique and everything," Halapio said. "[Harrison] should have [pancaked him]. He got in his way."

Florida offensive coordinator Brent Pease saw the play while reviewing game film on Sunday.

"Sometimes you have to laugh," he said, still chuckling and shaking his head in disbelief. "I mean, I'm just like, that is . . . c'mon."

"If I'd known I was going to live this long, I'd have taken better care of myself."
—*Mickey Mantle*

Once a Bonehead . . .

You can't put a price on all of the laughs we've shared while watching replays of the time that a ball bounced off Jose Canseco's head and over the wall for a home run.

You can, however, put a price on the cap that Canseco was wearing that day.

An auction listed the Texas Rangers cap Canseco was wearing when he misplayed a fly ball at the old Cleveland Stadium in a game in 1993. The ball bounced of Canseco's head and over the wall for a home run.

Canseco refuses to call the play a home run and insists on calling it a four-base error instead.

But I Was Only Going One Way

On June 23, 1963, veteran outfielder Jimmy Piersall stepped to the plate for the New York Mets facing Phillies pitcher Dallas Green to lead off the top of the fifth. Piersall swung on Green's offering and made solid contact—home run.

This wasn't just any homer for Piersall but a milestone homer. It was career homer No. 100, and he celebrated the milestone in a memorable fashion.

He decided to run around the bases backwards. Oh, he touched the bases in order: first, second, third, and home. That's not the part he did backwards. He just faced backwards. He backpedaled all the way around the infield.

"The Mets just had their first .500-or-better April since July of 1992."
—Ralph Kiner

Disco Fever

Bill Veeck was sixty-two years old—old enough to qualify for near-geezer—when he approved a promotion on July 12, 1979, that mocked disco music and incited a crowd of ninety thousand to trash Comiskey Park and storm the field, forcing umpires to declare a forfeit for the White Sox.

In the 1970s, the ubiquitous disco music craze annoyed many, including popular DJ Steve Dahl, who ranted against disco and blew up—symbolically anyway—disco records for radio station WLUP. Mike Veeck, son of White Sox owner Bill Veeck, who was famous for combining baseball with inventive publicity stunts, hatched the idea with Dahl and WLUP's station manager to cash in on the increasing hatred of disco with a Disco Demolition Night promotion. The event attracted an estimated ninety thousand people to the fifty-two thousand-seat stadium, leaving tens of thousands roaming around the stadium trying to get in. The smell of pot was in the air and the beer was flowing.

One reporter later wrote: "They were vulgarians who came to Comiskey Park to be ruffians."

The players completed the first game nervously as fans tossed records onto the field like Frisbees, or threw fireworks. With the crowd chanting "disco sucks," Dahl walked out to center field dressed in military regalia and set off an explosion of disco records. Many in the crowd took this as a cue to storm the field, and they began tearing up grass, scaling foul poles, starting fires, and overturning the batting cage.

The understaffed police were helpless. Veeck and (Harry) Caray pleaded for calm, and organist Nancy Faust played "Take Me Out to the Ballgame" to help quiet the crowd. Chicago police finally restored order after about 37 minutes, but the umpires ruled that the field was unplayable, forcing the White Sox to forfeit the second game.

> *"I may be dumb, but I'm not stupid."*
> —*Terry Bradshaw*

Beer's On Us, and You

In 1974 the Cleveland Indians staged ten-cent beer night: ten-ounce cups of beer for only ten cents at a game against the Texas Rangers. Management's senior moment? Forgetting that drunk people get crazy restless. More than twenty-five thousand fans showed up for the event, most of them already tipsy at the gate. Among the more tame incidents was a woman who flashed the crowd from the on-deck circle, a father-son team mooning the players, and fans jumping on the field to meet and shake hands with the outfielders. In the bottom of the ninth, the Indians tied the game, but never got a chance to win. Fans started throwing batteries, golf balls, cups and rocks onto the field and one even took the glove of the Rangers' right fielder. As the player rushed into the stands to get his glove back, fans starting swarming the field to stop him and threw chairs to block his way.

The Indians were forced to forfeit the game and nine fans were arrested. The AL president forced the franchise to abandon the promotion idea after understating "There was no question that beer played a great part in the affair." Really?

"Even Napoleon had his Watergate."
—*Danny Ozark*

Good Things to Throw

Los Angeles Dodgers fans in 1995 were treated to "ball night" for a game against the Cardinals. Fans entering the game were given a souvenir baseball. The senior moment? Forgetting that baseballs are pretty convenient things to throw. In the seventh inning, fans threw balls at an opposing outfielder when he bobbled a play. In the bottom of the ninth, though, Dodger Raul Mondesi and manager Tommy Lasorda were ejected for arguing a strikeout call, inspiring about two hundred fans to throw their promotional balls onto the field. The umps urged the Cardinals to stay on the field, but finally decided to end the game after more fans decided to contribute their gifts to the game.

The Dodgers were forced to forfeit the game, the first forfeit in the National League in forty-one years.

"The older I grow the more I distrust the familiar doctrine that age brings wisdom."
—*H. L. Mencken*

A Minor Mishap

In 2006 the West Michigan Whitecaps, Detroit's class-A affiliate, had a helicopter drop $1,000 in various bills from a helicopter after a game. The senior moment? Forgetting that people love money more than they love other people. Two children were injured scrambling for the cash. A girl received a bloody lip being pushed to the ground, while a seven-year-old boy was bruised when he got trampled in the fray.

The boy was taken to the hospital, but released after treatment. The team management summed up the incident by reminding everyone that they had signed waivers.

"I don't generally like running. I believe in training by rising gently up and down from the bench."
—Satchel Paige

A Big Fat Mistake

In 2007, the Dodgers decided to promote obesity by opening up a section of all-you-can-eat seats. Ticket prices ranged from $20–$40.

Our senior moment here? Failing to understand that not everyone can handle an open buffet of hot dogs and nachos. People ate themselves sick, literally.

Despite fans vomiting in their seats and elsewhere, the Dodgers declared the promotions a success and it still draws up to four thousand fans a night. Other stadiums have contacted the Dodgers about copying the idea.

The Incredible Satchel Paige, a Senior Champion

Though he played baseball for years and excelled, Satchel Paige's brief time in the major leagues includes what may be the most remarkable feat in baseball history. In 1965, at the age of fifty-nine, Paige (pitching for Charles Finley's Athletics), started a late-season against the Boston Red Sox and hurled three scoreless innings. Finley, a maverick of sorts, conceived the idea to sign and start Paige as a lark to boost the Athletics' sagging attendance. He gave Paige a $3,500 contract and Satchel immediately declared: "I think I can still pitch and help this club."

Finley, with considerable assistance from Paige, hyped the game masterfully. Before warming up, Paige sat in a rocking chair placed next to but not in the A's underground bullpen. Paige said: "At my age, I'm close enough to being below ground level as it is."

"He's a guy who gets up at six o'clock in the morning regardless of what time it is."
—*Lou Duva*

Working It, Part II

A white-uniformed nurse stood beside Paige to massage his arm before the game while a personal water boy handed him cool drinks.

Paige's six children looked on; his wife Lahoma, expecting a seventh child, stayed home. When the game began, Paige dominated. He recorded nine outs on only twenty-eight pitches and allowed just one hit, a double by Carl Yastrzemski. Ironically, during a Long Island semi-pro game a generation earlier, Yaz's father had hit against Paige.

Straight Talker

Journalists were interviewing Molly Holderness, a 103-year-old woman, "Tell us, Mrs. Holderness, what do you think is the best thing about being 103?" the reporter asked.

Molly smiled and looked straight at the reporter and simply replied, "No peer pressure."

Good Old Guy

George Blanda, a quarterback and place-kicker, played professional football longer than anyone else and retired having scored more points than anyone else. Blanda was a reliable kicker with a strong enough leg to have blasted a 55-yard field goal in 1961 and, nine years later, a 52-yarder. And he was a guileful, gutsy quarterback, a pocket passer who was never known for his arm strength or accuracy, his agility or his foot speed but who stood up to rushing linemen, saw the whole field, and often delivered his best performances when the most was at stake. "Blanda had a God-given killer instinct to make it happen when everything was on the line," Oakland Raiders owner Al Davis said. "I really believe that George Blanda is the greatest clutch player I have ever seen in the history of pro football."

Davis had a firsthand look at one of Blanda's most famous stretch of games when on Sunday, October 25, 1970, Blanda stepped in for the Raiders' injured starting quarterback, Daryle Lamonica, and threw for three touchdowns in the fourth quarter to beat Pittsburgh. The next Sunday, against the Kansas City Chiefs, he kicked a 48-yard field goal, salvaging a tie with eight seconds left in the game. The week after that, against the Cleveland Browns, Blanda entered the game with a little more than four minutes to play and the Raiders down by a touchdown. He threw a touchdown pass, kicked the extra point, drove the team into position for the winning field goal and kicked it— that 52-yarder—with three seconds on the clock. The next Sunday, he beat Denver with a late touchdown pass; the Sunday after that, he beat San Diego with a last-minute field goal. Five straight weeks he saved the game. He was forty-three years old at the time.

The Sporting News once wrote of Blanda, "He just got better. He was the epitome of the grizzled veteran, the symbol of everlasting youth."

A Little Pick-Me-Up

Cocaine can make you feel like you're virtually indestructible, which makes it a great pick for football players. One of the most visible abusers of Colombian marching powder in the late seventies was Dallas Cowboys strongside linebacker Thomas "Hollywood" Henderson, who already had a reputation for flamboyant antics.

Henderson would keep a liquid inhaler in his pants filled with a mixture of cocaine and water, which he would spray into his mouth throughout the game. Naturally, this made his behavior even more unpredictable, and during a game against the Redskins in 1979 Henderson actually stopped playing for a little while to wave handkerchiefs with the Cowboys logo at the cameras. He was fired from the team the next day.

"The advantage of a bad memory is that one enjoys several times the same good things for the first time."
—Friedrich Nietzsche

"Nothing is more responsible for the gold old days than a bad memory."
—Franklin P. Adams

Geezers at Play: The Top Ten Oldest Pros

1. Buddy Helms—87 years of age; auto racing
2. Fred Davis—78 years of age; snooker
3. Jerry Barber—77 years of age; golf
4. Raja Maharaj Singh—72 years of age; cricket
5. Skip Hall—64 years of age; mixed martial arts
6. Albert Beckles—61 years of age; bodybuilding
7. Saoul Mamby—60 years of age; boxing
8. Satchel Paige—59 years of age; baseball
9. Gordie Howe—52 years of age; hockey (tie)
10. Ron Jaworski—52 years of age; pro football (tie)

"I have five boys and they're all named George. If you want to be a good boxer, you have to prepare for memory loss."
—George Foreman

Smile for the Camera

After the 2008 Summer Olympics, Michael Phelps was one of the most famous athletes in the world. The gangly Maryland-born swimmer took home a staggering eight gold medals and was quickly paired with hot ladies and endorsement deals.

Unfortunately, Phelps also got close with wacky weed. In 2009, a photograph of him taking a power bong hit at a University of South Carolina party hit the British tabloids, and the world reacted in horror. Kellogg dropped him from sponsorship and he was fined by the USA Swimming organization.

Considering that weed is legal for personal use in several states now, it's kind of a shame that this is a big deal—it's not like he had reefer in his snorkel or anything.

But I Love the Fans

Apparently he liked having senior moments all the time. One of baseball's biggest stoners was Bernie Carbo, a designated hitter from Detroit who played on the totally drugged-out Red Sox team of the mid-1970s.

Carbo was a real character, traveling with a stuffed gorilla named Mighty Joe Young and once holding up a game against the Yankees for ten minutes so he could find a plug of chewing tobacco that fell out of his mouth.

Bernie was even high when he hit the three-run homer that helped the Sox tie up the 1975 World Series at 3–3. In 1978, when new Red Sox ownership hired a detective to find proof of his drug use, after just a day on the job the detective caught Carbo throwing base-balls into the stands for fans in exchange for baggies of marijuana.

Have to Quit Sometime

Retirement terrifies sports stars. The end of a stunning praise-filled career can feel like falling off a cliff to an athlete who thrives on fame and fortune. And the longer the career, the harder the end game seems to be. For living legends, it's especially tough to know how to quit. When World heavyweight champion Evander Holy-field turned fifty he still wanted to box professionally.

"I'm not retired," he says. "If I can get a champion-ship fight, I will."

He would not just fight anyone—only top boxers.

"I don't think there's anybody in this organization not focused on the 49ers . . . I mean Chargers."
—*Bill Belichick*

He Had a Nice Trip

Sometimes a brain freeze can produce surprising results. Dock Ellis was a fascinating figure, an outspoken and experimental pitcher for the Pittsburgh Pirates with a powerful arm. He also did something that no other baseball player has done—threw a no-hitter while peaking on LSD.

Ellis dropped the hallucinogen before a 1970 game against the San Diego Padres, believing that the team had the day off. When his girlfriend picked up a newspaper and discovered that not only were the Padres playing but Ellis was scheduled to start, he rushed off to the stadium still feeling the effects of the drug.

Ellis's pitching was wild that day—he walked eight batters and beaned one—but no batter managed to contact the ball and his no-hitter record stands.

Like Dying Twice

Kareem Abdul-Jabbar was one of the world's most famous basketball players. He remains the record all-time scorer in the National Basketball Association. He still has to duck to get his 7-foot, 2-inch frame through most doorways.

But when he retired as a player in 1989, after twenty years of professional play, he was at a loss.

"The first training camp that I missed, I was like, 'Jeez, what am I going to do now?'" He quoted another sports legend—Jackie Robinson—to describe how he felt when he retired.

"He said that athletes die twice," Abdul-Jabbar said. "You know, when that first career is gone, that's a death."

"All of us could take a lesson from the weather. It pays no attention to criticism."
—Anonymous

Irrelevance

Finding a passion off the court while she was still playing in major tournaments helped Martina Navratilova. When she was fifty-five the tennis superstar noted that after retiring, "you become irrelevant really quickly."

But because she never defined herself solely through tennis, she was able to accept the transition.

"My sense of self-worth did not depend on winning matches," she said. Instead she committed to keeping fit: she runs with her dogs, skis, cycles, and plays hockey. "And of course, I play tennis."

Navratilova serves as fitness ambassador for AARP, which she says she loves. Her advice to other athletes, professional and amateur? Play a new game when you get older.

"Find another sport that you can really improve at, that you can get excited about, and have fun," she said. Athletes can still satisfy their competitive drive, without comparing their current game to how they used to perform when they were younger.

"Nobody in the game of football should be called a genius. A genius is somebody like Norman Einstein."
—*Joe Montana*
"Hey, the offensive linemen are the biggest guys on the field, they're bigger than everybody else, and that's what makes them the biggest guys on the field."
—*John Madden*

Sex: Life is Sexually Transmitted

Many moralists would be inclined to say that sex has been causing problems forever, that without the various tensions and pretenses and extreme means everyone takes to participate, the world would be a much better place. But really. We all love sex, I think, and we all have at one time or another given it a shot. And would like to continue. None of us would be around without it.

"Age does not protect you from love. But love, to some extent, protects you from age."
—*Jeanne Moreau*

If Only I Could Remember

When I went to lunch today, I noticed an old man sitting on a park bench sobbing his eyes out. I stopped and asked him what was wrong.

He told me, "I have a twenty-two-year-old wife at home. She rubs my back every morning and then gets up and makes me pancakes, sausage, fresh fruit, and freshly ground coffee."

"Well, then why are you crying?" I asked.

He added, "She makes me homemade soup for lunch and my favorite biscuits, cleans the house and then watches sports TV with me for the rest of the afternoon."

I said, "Well, why are you crying?"

He said, "For dinner she makes me a gourmet meal with wine and my favorite dessert and then we cuddle until the small hours."

I inquired, "Well then, why in the world would you be crying?"

"I can't remember where I live."

"At my age, getting lucky means finding my car in the parking lot."
—Anonymous Old Fart

Plenty to Do

If you're not already depressed by how little action you've been getting lately, then you probably won't feel any better learning that people in their seventies and eighties are still sexually active a lot of the time. A study found up to 54 percent of men and 31 percent of women report having sex at least twice a month. Astounds? No. Remember that oldsters are still people.

Medical science is extending the human shelf life, which means people aren't spending their twilight years hunched over a bowl of porridge—they're actually *living*. And when their health permits, they can sometimes be found—but hopefully left alone—having sex. Researchers behind the study say doctors should consider this lifestyle trend in how they treat older patients.

*"First you forget names, then you forget faces.
Next you forget to pull your zipper up, and finally,
you forget to pull it down."*
—George Burns

Eat Elsewhere

An elderly couple was having trouble with their romantic lives. They visited the doctor who listened carefully, then pronounced his diagnosis.

"At your age," he stated, "you need spontaneity and immediacy. The next time you feel the urge, carry it out. I don't care if it's on the dining room table; take action."

The next month, the couple returned for their visit. "How did my suggestion work?" the doctor asked. "Great," the man replied, "but we can't eat at Shoneys' anymore."

Careful with the Meat

Andy Rooney, sage that he was, once observed: "Yes, we praise women over forty for a multitude of reasons. Unfortunately, it's not reciprocal. For every stunning, smart, well-coiffed, hot woman over forty, there is a bald, paunchy relic in yellow pants making a fool of himself with some twenty-two-year-old waitress. Ladies, I apologize. For all those men who say, 'Why buy the cow when you can get the milk for free?' here's an update for you. Nowadays eighty percent of women are against marriage. Why? Because women realize it's not worth buying an entire pig just to get a little sausage!"

"Those who love deeply never grow old; they may die of old age, but they die young."
—*Dorothy Canfield Fisher*

Ask Dr. Ruth

Dr. Ruth Westheimer wrote a book titled *Sex After 50*. "The important message really is to not give up. The idea in this country was: Why do older people engage in touching, or in arousal, or in sex? Grandchildren certainly think: My grandparents don't do *that*! So my message—if anybody tells me that's not what they want to do anymore, if anybody tells me, 'I've done it. I'm finished.'—is 'Wonderful. Go and read a good book.'

"But for those people who want to engage in that activity, they have to know not to engage in sex in the evening, when they are tired. But to engage in sex in the morning. Go for breakfast, go back into bed, because the testosterone level is highest in the morning. And also, if one of the partners at [a] later stage in life wants to have some sexual satisfaction, that's what they should engage in. If the other one doesn't want to, just lie there and think about the next meal."

"I'm at the age where food has taken the place of sex in my life. In fact, I've just had a mirror put over my kitchen table."
—Rodney Dangerfield

Still Alive

Not to rub it in, but another study, what some people called "unprecedented," emphasized again that many older people are surprisingly frisky—willing to do, and talk about, intimate acts that would make their grandchildren blush.

That may be too much information for some folks.

The most comprehensive sex survey ever done among fifty-seven to eight-five-year-olds in the United States found that sex and interest in it do fall off when people are in their seventies, but more than a quarter of those up to age eighty-five reported having sex in the previous year.

And the drop-off has a lot to do with health or lack of a partner, especially for women, the survey found.

Middle age ...

"Middle age is when you're faced with two temptations and you choose the one that will get you home by nine o'clock."
—Ronald Reagan

"Middle age is when you've met so many people that every new person you meet reminds you of someone else."
—Ogden Nash

"Middle age is when you still believe you'll feel better in the morning."
—Bob Hope

"Middle age occurs when you are too young to take up golf and too old to rush up to the net."
—Franklin P. Adams

"Middle age is a time when you discover you keep on growing older, even after you are old enough."
—Donald Raddle

"Middle Age: When you begin to exchange your emotions for symptoms."
—Georges Clemenceau

"Middle age is when you're sitting at home on a Saturday night and the telephone rings and you hope it isn't for you."
—Ogen Nash

"Middle age is having a choice between two temptations and choosing the one that'll get you home earlier."
—Dan Bennett

"Middle age is when your age starts to show around your middle."
—Bob Hope

Just Like a Baby

Two elderly gentlemen from a retirement center were sitting on a bench under a tree when one turned to the other and said:

"Slim, I'm 83 years old now, and I'm just full of aches and pains. I know you're about my age. How do you feel?"

Slim said, "I feel just like a newborn baby."

"Really!? Like a newborn baby?"

"Yep. No hair, no teeth, and I think I just wet my pants."

"Age is not important unless you're a cheese."
—Helen Hayes

Follow Their Example

Fruit flies with better sex lives live longer, a University of Michigan study found: aging and physiology are influenced by how the brain processes expectations and rewards.

It has long been accepted that for many species the expectation of food that does not become available shortens their lives. Now, researchers have found the same is true when it comes to expectations of sex that is denied. At least it appears to be true for male fruit flies.

Male fruit flies that perceived sexual interest from their female counterparts—without the opportunity to mate—experienced rapid decreases in fat stores, resistance to starvation and more stress. The sexually frustrated flies lived shorter lives.

Mating, on the other hand, partially reversed the negative effects on health and aging.

"I've been around so long, I knew Doris Day before she was a virgin."
—*Groucho Marx*

Listen to Your Doctor

Morris, an eighty-two-year-old man, went to the doctor to get a physical. A few days later the doctor saw Morris walking down the street with a gorgeous young woman on his arm.

A couple of days later the doctor spoke to Morris and said, "You're really doing great, aren't you?"

Morris replied, "Just doing what you said, Doc: 'Get a hot mamma and be cheerful.'"

The doctor said, "I didn't say that. I said, 'You've got a heart murmur. Be careful.'"

"Money and women. They're two of the strongest things in the world. The things you do for a woman you wouldn't do for anything else. Same with money."
—*Satchel Paige*

Don't Forget

An eighty-year-old couple are having problems remembering things, so they decide to see their doctor to find out if anything is wrong with them.

They see the doctor and tell him about the memory problems they've been having. After a check-up, the doctor tells them that they are physically fine but might want to start writing things down to help them remember. They thank the doctor and leave.

Later that night while watching TV, the old man gets up from his chair. "Where are you going?" asks his wife.

"To the kitchen," he replies.

"Will you get me a bowl of ice cream?" she asks.

"Sure," he says.

She says, "Maybe you should write it down so you'll remember."

"I'll remember," he says.

"Well, I would also like some strawberries on top," she adds. "You had better write that down cause I know you'll forget."

"I can remember that," he says, as he begins to lose his patience. "You want a bowl of ice cream with strawberries."

"I would also like whip cream on top," she adds. "I know you will forget so you better write it down."

Hopping mad he says "I don't need to write that down! I will remember just fine." He fumes into the kitchen to get the food.

After about twenty minutes he returns from the kitchen and hands her a plate of bacon and eggs. She stares at the plate for a moment and says, "You forgot my toast."

Confession

An elderly man goes into confession and says to the priest, "Father, I'm eighty years old, married, have four kids and eleven grandchildren. Last night I had an affair. I made love to two twenty-one-year-old girls. Both of them. Twice."

The priest said: "Well, my son, when was the last time you were in confession?"

"Never Father, I'm Jewish."

"So then, why are you telling me?"

"Are you kidding? I'm telling everybody!"

---

*"Millions long for immortality who do not
know what to do with themselves on a
rainy Sunday afternoon."*
—Susan Ertz

Senior Dating Ads

You can say what you want about Florida, but you never hear of anyone retiring and moving north. These are actual ads.

Foxy Lady

Sexy, fashion-conscious blue-haired beauty, 80s, slim, 5'4" (used to be 5'6"),

Searching for sharp-looking, sharp-dressing companion. Matching white shoes and belt a plus.

Long-Term Commitment

Recent widow who has just buried fourth husband, looking for someone to round out a six-unit plot. Dizziness, fainting, shortness of breath not a problem.

Serenity Now

I am into solitude, long walks, sunrises, the ocean, yoga and meditation. If you are the silent type, let's get together, take our hearing aids out and enjoy quiet times.

Winning Smile

Active grandmother with original teeth seeking
a dedicated flosser to share rare steaks,
corn on the cob, and caramel candy.

Beatles or Stones?

I still like to rock, still like to cruise in my Camaro on Saturday nights, and still like to play the guitar.

If you were a groovy chick, or are now a groovy hen, let's get together and listen to my eight-track tapes.

Memories

I can usually remember Monday through Thursday. If you can remember Friday, Saturday, and Sunday, let's put our two heads together.

Mint Condition

Male, 1932 model, high mileage, good condition, some hair, many new parts including hip, knee, cornea, valves. Isn't in running condition, but walks well.

Maybe a New Name Would Help with the Hubris?

Discredited New York Congressman Anthony Weiner tried to use a run for the mayor of New York City in 2013 as a way to resuscitate his political career. Weiner had stepped down from his congressional seat in 2011 after he admitted to sending sexual explicit photos to a woman he met online.

But Weiner's mayoral campaign ran into more problems. Weiner admitted later that that he continued to send explicit photos and texts a year after his resignation. During a mayoral campaign stop on Staten Island, a retired teacher questioned Weiner's "moral authority" to be mayor, telling Weiner, "Your standard of conduct is so much lower than the standard of conduct that's expected of me."

Later, on the first day of Rosh Hashanah, a Jewish voter confronted Weiner outside a Brooklyn bakery, with Weiner asking repeatedly "you're my judge?" The man told Weiner, "You talk to God, you work out your problems, but stay out of the public eye." Weiner responded, "I've fought very hard for this community and delivered more than you will ever in your entire life."

Weiner ended up staying in the mayoral race but came in fifth in the Democratic primary.

Stipulations

An elderly couple reaching their seventies are about to get married, but before they say their vows, the woman wanted to talk.

She said: "I want to keep my house."

He said: "That's fine with me."

She said: "I want to keep my Cadillac."

He said: "That's fine with me."

She said: "And I want to have sex six times a week."

He said: "Put me down for Fridays."

"Sex at age ninety is like trying to shoot pool with a rope."
—*George Burns*

Question: How many days in a week?
Answer: Six Saturdays, one Sunday.

Not Hungry

A little old lady was running up and down the halls in a nursing home. As she walked, she would flip up the hem of her nightgown and say "Supersex."

She walked up to an elderly man in a wheelchair. Flipping her gown at him, she said, "Supersex."

He sat silently for a moment or two and finally answered, "I'll take the soup."

"A dirty book is rarely dusty."
—Anonymous

Good Timing

"My grandfather just died. In a way I'm quite proud of him. He died having sex with my grandma, he is ninety-three years old and was getting his thing on. Anyways my grandma said 'We were doing it on Sunday morning, it was Sunday cause he could use the church bells to pace himself.' I think he would be alive today if an ice cream van hadn't gone past."—Mitlancer

That's Why

A ninety-seven-year-old man goes into his doctor's office and says, "Doc, I want my sex drive lowered." "Sir," replied the doctor, "you're ninety-seven. Don't you think your sex drive is all in your head?" "You're damned right it is!" replied the old man. "That's why I want it lowered!"

"If sex is such a natural phenomenon, how come there are so many books on how to do it?"
—Bette Midler

Heavenly Rewards

Sylvia: Hi! Wanda.

Wanda: Hi! Sylvia.
How'd you die?

Sylvia: I froze to death.

Wanda: How horrible!

Sylvia: It wasn't so bad. After I quit shaking from the cold, I began to get warm and sleepy, and finally died a peaceful death.
What about you?

Wanda: I died of a massive heart attack. I suspected that my husband was cheating, so I came home early to catch him in the act. But instead, I found him all by himself in the den watching TV.

Sylvia: So, what happened?

Wanda: I was so sure there was another woman there somewhere that I started running all over the house looking.

I ran up into the attic and searched, and down into the basement. Then I went through every closet and checked under all the beds. I kept this up until I had looked everywhere, and finally I became so exhausted that I just keeled over with a heart attack and died.

Sylvia: Too bad you didn't look in the freezer—we'd both still be alive.

"Old age, believe me, is a good and pleasant thing. It is true you are gently shouldered off the stage, but then you are given such a comfortable front stall as spectator."
—*Confucius*

At the Gym

Let's face it, working out is a pain in the ass and exercise is overrated. But I would reluctantly have to admit that there is no small amount of evidence that exercise and eating nutritious foods, and skipping that fourth lunchtime martini, have their benefits. Some people have even thrived.

"Be careful about reading health books.
You may die of a misprint."
—Mark Twain

Get Going

A one hundred-year-old Japanese woman became the world's first centenarian to complete a 1,500-meter freestyle swim, twenty years after she took up the sport.

Mieko Nagaoka took just under an hour and sixteen minutes to finish the race as the sole competitor in the 100–104-year-old category at a short course pool in Ehime, western Japan.

"I want to swim until I turn 105 if I can live that long," the sprightly Nagaoka told *Kyodo News*.

"Good health is merely the slowest possible rate at which
one can die."
—Samuel Johnson

Not So Fast There, Hidekichi

Sprinter Hidekichi Miyazaki, who was 103 when he nailed down the world record for the 100-meter dash in the 100–104 age category, clocking up a respectable 29.83 seconds.

His late-blooming athletic prowess has seen him dubbed "Golden Bolt"—a reference to Jamaican sprinter Usain Bolt.

"Those who think they have not time for bodily exercise will sooner or later have to find time for illness."
—Edward Stanley, the Earl of Derby, 1873

The Comeback Kid

Roy Rodriques, a ninety-year-old Connecticut resident, is determined to resume his career as one of the nation's top senior athletes after a stroke and a heart attack in 2014. The nonagenarian, who speaks in the forceful, booming voice of a much younger man, acknowledges his days as a dominating senior sprinter are probably over. But there's still the field part of track and field. "I'm going now to the fields. Shot put, discus, high jump!"

When Rodriques retired in the early 1980s, he decided to compete in senior track and field events. As he aged, he began to dominate. He figures he's won more than 100 medals in the 100, 200, and 400 meters, as well as the high jump, the triple jump, and other events.

"I have a two-story house and a bad memory, so I'm up and down those stairs all the time. That's my exercise."
—Betty White

A Thought on Health

Health nuts are going to feel stupid someday, lying in the hospital, dying of nothing.

"Dying is the last thing I want to do."
—Anonymous

"None are so old as those who have outlived enthusiasm."
—Henry David Thoreau

Take Your Time

"I feel like my body has gotten totally out of shape, so I got my doctor's permission to join a fitness club and start exercising. I decided to take an aerobics class for pensioners [seniors]. I bent, twisted, gyrated, jumped up and down, and perspired for an hour. But, by the time I got my leotard on, the class was over."

"Men are like wine: Some turn to vinegar, but the best improve with age."
—Pope John XXIII

Rose Is a Rose

An elderly couple had dinner at another couple's house, and after eating, the wives left the table and went into the kitchen.

The two elderly gentlemen were talking, and one said, "Last night we went out to a new restaurant and it was really great. I would recommend it very highly."

CHAPTER FIVE | 107

The other man said, "What's the name of the restaurant?"

The first man knits his brow in obvious concentration, and finally said to his companion, "Aahh, what is the name of that red flower you give to someone you love?"

His friend replies, "A carnation?"

"No. No. The other one," the man says.

His friend offers another suggestion, "The poppy?"

"Nahhhh," growls the man. "You know the one that is red and has thorns."

His friend said, "Do you mean a rose?"

"Yes, yes that's it. Thank you!" the first man says.

He then turns toward the kitchen and yells, "Rose, what's the name of that restaurant we went to last night?"

"Well, I tell you, if I have been wrong in my agnosticism,
when I die I'll walk up to God in a manly way and say,
Sir, I made an honest mistake."
—*H. L. Mencken*

I'll Drink to That

Faukja Singh at 101 is the oldest person ever to complete a marathon, as in 26.2 miles, as in running. He finished the Toronto Waterfront Marathon in 8 hours and 11 minutes. In 2003 when he was a mere 93 years old, he completed the same marathon in just 5 hours and 40 minutes, a time most young adults would be proud of.

Singh is a latecomer to the sport. He took up long-distance running his eighties as a way to cope with the tragic deaths of his wife and son. He's celebrated in the running world, and even carried the Olympic Torch during pre-celebrations for the London Olympics. He attributes his good health to a vegetarian diet and the avoidance of alcohol and tobacco.

"Age is an issue of mind over matter. If you don't mind, it doesn't matter."
—Mark Twain

Get to the Top

And what could be more challenging and sublime than Everest, the tallest mountain in the world? Each year, hundreds of climbers head to Everest to attempt the summit and only a fraction make it to the top. And inevitably some perish during the journey. But the prospect of failure and the very real risks did not deter Min Bahadur Sherchan.

At age seventy-six Sherchan became the oldest person to summit the 29,000-foot peak, male or female. She told reporters that she was climbing for a better world, remarking, "My main objective for climbing Everest was for world peace. I was determined to either climb the peak or die trying." Her journey nearly ended in disaster when unexpected winds lashed the mountain during her ascent; but Sherchan persevered and cemented a spot in the record books.

Ninety—Count Them—World Records

Don Pellman of Santa Monica, California, is one of the most successful elderly track athletes in the world. He holds practically every American track and field record imaginable for the over-90 group, including long jump, high jump, discus, the 100 meter dash, triple jump and javelin throw. He also holds a number of

90+ *world* records. He attributes his good health to a common sense, healthy diet and suggests that people who want to stay in shape never use the elevator, but take the stairs instead, noting "I think most people don't exercise enough."

"Don't send me flowers when I'm dead. If you like me, send them while I'm alive."
—Brian Clough

Remember This: Eat Well

A recent report has noted you can avoid the memory lapses that affect so many of us older citizens by staying hydrated and eating select foods. Imagine that? The study monitored the eating habits of nearly thirty thousand participants in some forty countries over five years. In one word: superfoods. A superfood is easy to find in the grocery store, contains nutrients that are known to enhance longevity, and has other health benefits that are backed by peer-reviewed, scientific studies.

Among the highlights:

> Drinking green tea will increase your metabolism, which will burn more fat. And the antioxidants found in green tea can help prevent cancer.

> Any type of whole grain in your diet—from barley to brown rice—will aid in weight loss by filling you up for fewer calories.

> Low-fat dairy is an important part of any superfood-focused diet. Yogurt in particular helps reduce the production of cortisol, a hormone that can slow metabolism.

> Beans, beans, and more beans. Black, kidney, white and garbanzo beans (also known as

chickpeas) all end up on superfood lists because of their fiber and protein. They fill you up and provide muscle-building material without any of the fat that meat can add to your meal.

➤ Popeye knew. Spinach is a great source of iron, which is a key component in red blood cells that fuel our muscles with oxygen for energy.

➤ Walnuts are packed with tryptophan, an amino acid your body needs to create the feel-great chemical serotonin.

➤ Asparagus is one of the best veggie sources of folate, a B vitamin that could help keep you out of the mental doldrums.

➤ Broccoli makes the list because it's one of nature's most nutrient-dense foods, with only 30 calories per cup. That means you get a ton of hunger-curbing fiber and polyphenols—anti-oxidants that detoxify cell-damaging chemicals in your body—with each serving.

*"Age appears to be best in four things: old wood
to burn, old wine to drink, old friends to trust,
and old authors to read."*
—Francis Bacon

*"Just remember: Once you're over the hill, you begin to
pick up speed."*
—Arthur Schopenhauer

*"A man knows when he is growing old because he begins
to look like his father."*
—Gabriel Garcia Marquez, Love in the Time of Cholera

*"In youth the days are short and the years are old. In old
age the years are short and day's long."*
—Pope Paul VI

"Age is a very high price to pay for maturity."
—Tom Stoppard

*"One of the many things nobody ever tells you about middle
age is that it's such a nice changes from being young."*
—William Feather

Epitaphs and Funerals: The Ultimate Senior Moments

EPITAPHS AND FUNERALS: THE ULTIMATE SENIOR MOMENTS

It's going to happen to all of us eventually. At some point in our lives—hopefully later than sooner—we will all croak. My own thought is that when it does, why not go out in style and with a message that might make people smile and think. Your epitaph (the word means "on the grave" in ancient Greek) might be the first time you have had done that.

"We are born naked, wet, and hungry.
Then things get worse"
—Bumper sticker

"Life's a beach, and then you drown."
—Anonymous

"Either this man is dead or my
watch has stopped."
—Groucho Marx in A Day at the Races

"I have never killed a man, but I have read many
obituaries with a lot of pleasure."
—Clarence Darrow

Woulda, Coulda, Shoulda

When I was young and free and my imagination had no limits, I dreamed of changing the world.

As I grew older and wiser, I discovered the world would not change, so I shortened my sights somewhat and decided to change only my country.

But it, too, seemed immovable.

As I grew into my twilight years, in one last desperate attempt, I settled for changing only my family, those closest to me, but alas, they would have none of it.

And now, as I lie on my deathbed, I suddenly realize: If I had only changed myself first, then by example I would have changed my family.

From their inspiration and encouragement, I would then have been able to better my country, and who knows, I may have even changed the world.

—Written on the tomb of an Anglican Bishop in Westminster Abby

Prices Are Killing Me

True story: A woman whose mother had died described making the funeral arrangements and kept cracking up while telling the story. Her mother expressed a wish for the cheapest coffin and fittings available because she wanted to be cremated. Her daughter went to the funeral home and chose a coffin to accommodate her mother's last wish. There were two options for pillows, one $5 the other $20. "What's the difference?" she asked. "The higher priced pillows don't need ironing," the funeral director said.

"A star on earth—a star in heaven."
—Karen Carpenter

"I like to look on the bright side: Every day I beat my own previous record for number of consecutive days I've stayed alive."
—Scott Frank

"I never thought about heaven per se. I think when you're dead, you're dead. If anything happens after that, you just hope you don't go to hell."
—Helen Thomas

Seen on a Headstone

"Now I know something you don't."
—Anonymous

"He died in bed."
—Tombstone of renowned gunfighter Doc Holliday

"I told you I was sick."
—Tombstone of Spike Milligan

"I'm in on a plot."
—Tombstone of Alfred Hitchcock

"I am ready to meet my Maker. Whether my Maker is prepared for the great ordeal of meeting me is another matter."
—Tombstone of Winston Churchill

"He enjoyed booze, guns, cars, and younger women until the day he died."
—Tombstone of Mike "Flathead" Blanchard

"My tombstone? I'm thinking something along the lines of 'Geez, he was just here a minute ago.'"
—George Carlin

"When I was young and free and my imagination had no limits, I dreamed of changing the world.
As I grew older and wiser, I discovered the world would not change, so I shortened my sights somewhat and decided to change only my country.
But it, too, seemed immovable.
As I grew into my twilight years, in one last desperate attempt, I settled for changing only my family, those closest

to me, but alas, they would have none of it.
And now, as I lie on my deathbed, I suddenly realize:
If I had only changed myself first, then by example
I would have changed my family.
From their inspiration and encouragement, I would then
have been able to better my country, and who knows,
I may have even changed the world."
—Written on the tomb of an Anglican Bishop in
Westminster Abby

"I've just read that I am dead. Don't forget to delete me
from your list of subscribers."
—Rudyard Kipling, writing to a magazine that had
mistakenly published an announcement of his death

"Here lies a man who knew how to enlist the service of
better men than himself."
—Tombstone of Andrew Carnegie

"That's All Folks!"
—Epitaph of Mel Blanc, the Man of a Thousand Voices

"I will not be right back after this message."
—Tombstone of Merv Griffin

"There goes the neighborhood."
—*Tombstone of Rodney Dangerfield*

"I had a lover's quarrel with the world."
—*Tombstone of Robert Frost*

"So we beat on, boats against the current,
borne back ceaselessly
into the past."
—The Great Gatsby, *from the tombstone of F. Scott*
Fitzgerald

"This Grave
contains all that was Mortal
of a
Young English Poet
Who
on his Death Bed
in the Bitterness of his Heart
at the Malicious Power of his Enemies
Desired
these words to be engraved on his Tomb Stone:
"Here lies One Whose Name was writ in Water."'
—*Tombstone of John Keats*

"Quoth the raven, 'Nevermore.'"
—Tombstone of Edgar Allan Poe

"The reason so many people showed up at his funeral was because they wanted to make sure he was dead."
—Samuel Goldwyn, referring to fellow film producer Louis B. Mayer

"Always go to other people's funerals, otherwise they won't come to yours."
—Yogi Berra

"Why is it that we rejoice at a wedding and cry at a funeral? It is because we are not the person involved."
—Mark Twain

"I think you should live your life so that the maximum number of people will attend your funeral."
—Scott Adams

"The first thing you should do when you get up is read the obituaries. You never know when you'll see a name that will just make your day."
—Ed Salisbury

"They say such nice things about people at their funerals that it makes me sad to realize that I'm going to miss mine by just a few days."
—Garrison Keillor

"At Rest
An American Soldier
And Defender of the Constitution"
—Tombstone of Jefferson Davis

"Funeral: a pageant whereby we attest our respect for the dead by enriching the undertaker, and strengthen our grief by an expenditure that deepens our groans and doubles our tears."
—Ambrose Bierce

"Nobody will say on their deathbed: 'I wish I had spent more time in the office.'"
—Anonymous

"You know your life is over when you own a lawnmower."
—Todd Skinner

"When you were born, you cried, and the world rejoiced. Live your life in such a manner that

when you die, the world cries and
you rejoice."
—*Indian Proverb*

"All stories, if continued far enough, end in death."
—*Ernest Hemingway*

"Let us so live that when we come to die even the
undertaker will be sorry."
—*Mark Twain*

"The Best Is Yet To Come."
—*Tombstone of Frank Sinatra*

"The Entertainer
He did it all"
—*Tombstone of Sammy Davis Jr.*

". . . that nothing's so sacred as honor and nothing's
so loyal as love"
—*Tombstone of Wyatt Earp*

"The Body of B. Franklin, Printer; like the
Cover of an old Book, Its Contents torn out,

EPITAPHS AND FUNERALS: THE ULTIMATE SENIOR MOMENTS

And stript of its Lettering and Gilding, Lies here,
Food for Worms.
But the Work shall not be wholly lost; For it will, as he
believ'd, appear once more, In a new & more perfect
Edition, Corrected and amended By the Author."
—Tombstone of Benjamin Franklin

"Murdered By A Traitor and A Coward Whose
Name Is Not Worthy To Appear Here"
—Tombstone of Jesse James

"The mortal remains of Ethan Allen,
fighter, writer, statesman, and philosopher,
lie in this cemetery beneath the marble statue.
His spirit is in Vermont now."
—Tombstone of Ethan Allen

"Truth and History.
21 Men.
The Boy Bandit King—
He Died As He Lived."
—Tombstone of William H. Bonney, Billy the Kid

"My Jesus Mercy"
—Tombstone of Alphonse "Al" Capone

Politics

A well-known journalist once wrote that the biggest gaffe a politician can make is telling the truth. If that were true, there would be very few gaffes. It seems politics, politicians, and jaw-dropping senior moments go together like soup and sandwiches or Larry, Curly, and Moe. The marriage of politics and doltishness has been a solid one since the first man ran for office, to the point that saying "dumb politician" is very close to redundant. Pointing this out is not unlike shooting fish in a barrel.

"Old age is no place for sissies."
—Bette Davis

Imagine That

The mayor of a California city struggling with a spike in burglaries and other crimes has apologized for promoting a class about how to pick locks in her newsletter.

Oakland Mayor Jean Quan said Wednesday she understood the reaction of people who were upset about a listing for the lock-picking class. She said she will do a better job reviewing listings in the future.

The class—offered through the website, work-shopweekend.net—was geared toward people who misplace their keys. But it didn't go over well with some residents given the city's crime woes, including a more than forty percent jump in burglaries last year.

"As I grow older, I pay less attention to what men say. I just watch what they do."
—Andrew Carnegie

Mind Like a Steel Trap

Texas Governor Rick Perry, on a quest for the Republican Presidential nomination, had a slight setback in a televised debate in front of millions.

Perry tried to name the three federal agencies he would like to eliminate if he is elected president, but he was able to name just two: the Commerce and Education Departments.

Perry received some assistance from fellow candidate Ron Paul, who suggested that he should actually eliminate five agencies. At another point in the debate, someone else helpfully suggested that perhaps Perry was talking about the Environmental Protection

Agency. He said that agency wasn't it, and ended with a simple, "Oops."

"Our enemies are innovative and resourceful, and so are we. They never stop thinking about new ways to harm our country and our people, and neither do we."
—George W. Bush

Honesty Is Not the Best Policy

You only get one chance to make a first impression. But after the 1992 vice-presidential debate, Admiral James Stockdale was begging for a second. During his introduction, Stockdale began by saying, "Who am I, why am I here? I'm not a politician, everybody knows that . . ." This moment of honesty—followed by his unfocused performance during the debate—led voters to believe that Stockdale was in over his head. His joke tanked, and instead he became a national punch line.

"Old minds are like old horses; you must exercise them if you wish to keep them in working order."
—John Adams

From the Master Forgetter

Ronald Reagan was never particularly admired for his memory. In 1992, three years after leaving the White

House, Reagan's forgetting became impossible to ignore. He was eighty-one.

In his stable of disarming jokes were several about memory troubles afflicting the elderly. He shared one at a 1985 dinner honoring Senator Russell Long:

"An elderly couple was getting ready for bed one night," Reagan told the crowd. "The wife turned to her husband and said, 'I'm just so hungry for ice cream and there isn't any in the house.'

"'I'll get you some,' her husband offered.

"'You're a dear,' she said. 'Vanilla with chocolate sauce. Write it down—you'll forget.'

"'I won't forget,' he said.

"'With whipped cream on top.'

"'Vanilla with chocolate sauce and whipped cream on top,' he repeated.

"'And a cherry,' she said.

"'And a cherry on top.'

"'Please write it down,' she said. 'I know you'll forget.'

"'I won't forget,' he insisted. 'Vanilla with chocolate sauce, whipped cream, and a cherry on top.'"

"The husband went off and returned after a while with a paper bag, which he handed to his wife in bed. She opened up the bag, and pulled out a ham sandwich.

"'I told you to write it down,' she said. 'You forgot the mustard.'"

Remember the Alamo . . .

Texas Governor Greg Abbott recently stood by his decision to order the state guard to monitor the US military amid fears from conspiracy theorists that an upcoming training exercise is really an attempt to take over the state.

Abbott, who issued a letter to the Texas State Guard ordering it to oversee the US military training operation known as "Jade Helm 15," said his decision was an attempt to function as a "communication facilitator" between the military and Texans concerned about the program.

Jade Helm 15 has been described by the military as a "standard training exercise," but conspiracy theorists have said the operation may be an attempt by the federal government to stage a military takeover of Texas.

"Old age is like everything else. To make a success of it, you've got to start young."
—*Theodore Roosevelt*

"Probably the happiest period in life most frequently is in middle age, when the eager passions of youth are cooled, and the infirmities of age not yet begun; as we see that the shadows, which are at morning and evening so large, almost entirely disappear at midday."
—*Eleanor Roosevelt*

Chuck Does . . .

Chuck Norris, actor and conservative icon, has offered his two cents on whether or not President Obama plans to invade certain parts of Texas under the guise of "military training exercises," and has firmly stood up for the side that says "Yes, that sounds entirely plausible."

Conservative media was consumed with talk that the Jade Helm 15 military training exercise scheduled to take place this summer was really a cover for a hostile takeover of Republican areas of the South deemed by the Obama administration as *maybe a bit too patriotic.*

"Old age is the only disease you don't look forward to being cured of."
—Citizen Kane

Motor City Blues

Boston Mayor Thomas M. Menino was once asked during an interview with the *New York Times* magazine what other city he'd like to live in. He responded, "Detroit is a place I'd love to go." When asked what he would do in Detroit, Menino said: "I'd blow up the place and start all over. No, seriously, when it takes a police officer ninety minutes to answer a call, there's something wrong with the system." Menino later had to apologize after Detroit Mayor Dave Bing said Menino was insensitive.

"A diplomat is a man who always remembers a woman's birthday but never remembers her age."
—*Robert Frost*

But He Didn't Inhale

Canadian politics and politicians tend to get little attention in the United States. That changed dramatically after Toronto mayor Rob Ford admitted he had smoked crack cocaine. Allegations of the mayor's drug use came up after a video surfaced showing Ford smoking crack. Ford denied the video existed until police said they had obtained a copy in the course of a drug investigation against a friend of Ford's.

"Yes, I have smoked crack cocaine, " Ford later told reporters. "There have been times when I've been in a drunken stupor. That's why I want to see the tape."

Bearings, or Marbles?

Seventy-two-year-old John McCain is the oldest person in US history to run for the presidency, when his opponent Barack Obama was forty-six. During the campaign Obama once accused McCain of "losing his bearings," a polite way of saying that McCain is becoming senile. McCain, in turn, sometimes referred to Obama as "that young man with very little experience."

> *"Old age is like a plane flying through a storm. Once you're aboard, there's nothing you can do."*
> —*Golda Meir*

Oh, That Ron, Part II

From a speech: "I have three things that I want to tell you today. The first is that I seem to be having a little problem with my memory. I cannot remember the other two."

It Was More of a *Señor* Moment

Senator John McCain once had what many called a bizarre interview with a Spanish language radio station in Miami. During his talk he repeatedly gave vague answers about Latin America when asked about President José Luis Rodríguez Zapatero of Spain.

In Spain, there seemed to be a specific line of thinking. The great majority appeared to think the McCain was simply confused and didn't know who Zapatero was—something you might bone up on if you were about to do an interview with the Spanish press. The assumption seems to be that since he'd already been asked about Castro and Chavez, McCain assumed Zapatero must be some other Latin American bad guy.

"It's scary when you start making the same noises as your coffee maker."
—Anonymous

Uncle Joe

Vice President Joe Biden has stopped surprising people with his impolitic and spontaneous expressions.

During a White House St. Patrick's Day celebration, he briefly mourned the death of the Irish Prime Minister's mother, even though she was very much alive. After he introduced President Barack Obama during the signing of a health bill, he turned to the president, unaware he was wearing a live microphone and said, "This is a big f—— deal." With his use of the *F* word, Biden offered the ultimate blue-collar acknowledgment of a job well done. White House press secretary Robert Gibbs quickly came to the Vice President's defense with a simple note on his official Twitter feed: "And yes, Mr. Vice President, you're right . . ."

Let's Face It, She's Hot

During a Democratic fundraiser in Silicon Valley, President Barack Obama commended California Attorney General Kalama Harris, saying, "She's brilliant and she's dedicated, she's tough." He then added, "She also happens to be, by far, the best-looking attorney general." As the crowd laughed, he continued, "It's true! C'mon."

He later had to apologize, with his press secretary Jay Carney saying that the president did not want to diminish Harris's professional accomplishments and abilities.

Carney did not mention what Michelle had to say.

I Sort Of Meant It

President Barack Obama had promised Americans multiple times that they would be allowed to keep their insurance if they liked it under the Affordable Care Act, also known as Obamacare. So when insurance companies sent out hundreds of thousands of cancellation notices for noncompliant plans in October and November, it created a political furor. The president later took the blame at a press conference, saying, "With respect to the pledge I made that if you like your plan you can keep it, the way I put that forward unequivocally ended up not being accurate."

"If we do everything right, if we do it with absolute certainty, there's still a 30 percent chance we're going to get it wrong."
—*Joe Biden*

Wishy Washy? Maybe I Am, Maybe I'm Not

Under attack for changing his mind on important issues for political reasons, Democratic presidential candidate John Kerry explained his switch on a funding bill. "I actually did vote for the $87 billion, before I voted against it," he declared. That one sentence came to define the Massachusetts senator in the minds of many swing voters. Republican National Convention attendees taunted Kerry by waving flip-flops on the Madison Square Garden convention floor. Republicans repeated the ad from coast to coast. Kerry came close but fell just short of unseating President George W. Bush.

Try Me

When rumors first began circulating in 1987 that Democratic presidential frontrunner Gary Hart was having affairs, he taunted the press. "Follow me around," he challenged the media. "It will be boring." Well, they did. And it wasn't boring. The *Miami Herald* discovered a woman named Donna Rice. The famous *National Enquirer* photos on the good ship *Monkey Business* followed. And Hart—whose campaign buttons stated "My Heart Belongs to Gary"—ended up jilted by voters.

"Hillary Clinton is as qualified or more qualified than I am to be Vice President of the United States of America. Let's get that straight. She's a truly close personal friend. She is qualified to be President of the United States of America. She's easily qualified to be Vice President of the United States of America. Quite frankly, it might have been a better pick than me. But she's first rate."
—Joe Biden, suggesting Obama's former rival

Hands On Prez

Keep your hands to yourself, Mr. President.

Aside from seeming rude, inappropriate, and slightly sexist, President George W. Bush's shoulder rub to German Chancellor Angela Merkel, captured on film and video for all to enjoy, was a sight many people tried to forget. It was not one of Bush's most mature moments and the move seems a bit more appropriate to a fourth-grade lunchroom than a meeting of heads of state.

What's in a Word?

Are you from Poland? Then President Jimmy Carter wants to sleep with you. That's what his translator, Steven Seymour, told the then-Communist country during the US President's 1977 visit. Carter said he wanted to learn about the Polish people's desires for the future; Seymour said that Carter desired the Poles. Carter said he was happy to be in Poland; Seymour said he was happy to grasp at Poland's private parts. Carter talked about leaving the US to go on a trip; Seymour said that he had abandoned America forever. Then he spoke Russian—to a nation struggling under the thumb of the Soviet Union.

A Stream of Senior-Moment Wisdom from George W.

"I promise you I will listen to what has been said here, even though I wasn't here."
—*At the President's Economic Forum in Waco, Texas, August 13, 2002*

"We spent a lot of time talking about Africa, as we should. Africa is a nation that suffers from incredible disease."
—Gothenburg, Sweden, June 14, 2001

"You teach a child to read, and he or her will be able to pass a literacy test."
—Townsend, Tennessee, February 21, 2001

"Tribal sovereignty means that; it's sovereign. I mean, you're a—you've been given sovereignty, and you're viewed as a sovereign entity. And therefore the relationship between the federal government and tribes is one between sovereign entities."
—Washington, D.C., August 6, 2004

"I glance at the headlines just to kind of get a flavor for what's moving. I rarely read the stories, and get briefed by people who are probably read the news themselves."
—Washington, D.C., September 21, 2003

"The war on terror involves Saddam Hussein because of the nature of Saddam Hussein, the history of Saddam Hussein, and his willingness to terrorize himself."
—Grand Rapids, Michigan, January 29, 2003

"This foreign policy stuff is a little frustrating."
—As quoted by the New York Daily News, April 23, 2002

"I couldn't imagine somebody like Osama bin Laden understanding the joy of Hanukkah."
—At a White House menorah lighting ceremony, Washington, D.C., December 10, 2001

"For every fatal shooting, there were roughly three non-fatal shootings. And, folks, this is unacceptable in America. It's just unacceptable. And we're going to do something about it."
—Philadelphia, Pennsylvania, May 14, 2001

"There's an old saying in Tennessee—I know it's in Texas, probably in Tennessee—that says, fool me once, shame on—shame on you. Fool me—you can't get fooled again."
—Nashville, Tennessee, September. 17, 2002

Unbelievably Dumb

Secretary of State John Kerry found himself having to explain his remarks on a possible US military intervention in Syria. As the White House was laying out an ultimatum against the Bashir Assad regime, Kerry promised during a press conference in London that the planned US intervention would be an "unbelievably small, limited kind of effort." Opponents of US intervention in Syria seized on the remark. Senator John McCain posted on Twitter, "Kerry says #Syria would be 'unbelievably small'—that is unbelievably unhelpful." Jay Carney, the president's press secretary, said that Kerry was contrasting possible military action in Syria with operations in Afghanistan and Iraq.

Adding to the confusion over Kerry's remark on the size of a planned US attack was his giving an unexpected out to the Assad regime, an out that the White House apparently didn't know about. When asked how Assad could avert a US attack, Kerry said, "[Assad] could turn over every single bit of his chemical weapons to the international community in the next week, turn it over, all of it, without delay, and allow the full and total accounting for that, but he isn't about to do it." Kerry's proposal, the White House said, was intended to be rhetorical.

Inspirations

I'm more inclined to admire Ambrose Bierce and H. L. Mencken than I am the folks who write the sappy aphorisms found on Hallmark greeting cards, but even I do get inspired sometimes by the efforts of those oldsters among us who have forgotten they're supposed to be sitting in a rocking chair and drooling away their last years. Sometimes I think it's not such a bad thing to be an old guy.

Not Too Late

Mary Wesley had her first novel, *Jumping the Queue*, published when she was seventy.

"My mom used to say, 'The best thing about having Alzheimer's or dementia is that every day is brand new —this is a no baggage flight!'"

Not the Retiring Type

Florence Rigney can't see why a lot of people want to retire at age sixty. She tried, but it lasted only five months.

Now ninety, she's the United States' oldest practicing nurse, still wandering the halls of Tacoma General Hospital in Washington, setting up the operating room and making her fellow nurses smile.

"She runs circles around all of us," Sheri Morris, assistant nurse manager, said. "She's a wealth of wisdom and knowledge, and we absolutely love her."

Morris and her director decided to have a celebration as Rigney began her seventh decade of work.

"We had to do something," Morris said. "She'd had over six decades of service at the hospital. How could we not honor that?"

"Retirement at sixty-five is ridiculous. When I was sixty-five I still had pimples."
—George Burns

Not Fried

Colonel Sanders (real name Harland Sanders) started his KFC empire at the age of sixty-five. He had previously worked as a farmhand, an army mule-tender, and a locomotive fireman.

"People can get crazier as they get older. I can just be weird whenever I want, and there's the freedom of not caring what people think."
—Candace Bergen

You Won't Be Alone

More than 53,000 centenarians live in the US, with 330 of them reaching "super-centenarian" status, or turning 110 or older, according to the 2010 census. Celebrating your 100th birthday isn't that rare anymore, with the number of US centenarians growing 65 percent since 1980.

"When I was younger I'd berate myself: You're fat, you're not a good dancer, you'll never have a boyfriend. I don't sweat that kind of stuff anymore. Now every day is a miracle. I've also learned that if something is painful or upsetting, you shouldn't hide from it. You should make it part of your life instead."
—Valerie Harper

A Different Perspective

It was December of 1914 when Thomas Edison's great laboratories in West Orange, New Jersey, were almost entirely destroyed by fire. In one night Edison lost $2 million worth of equipment and the record of much of his life's work. Edison's son Charles ran frantically about trying to find his father and finally came upon him standing near the fire, his face ruddy in the glow, and his white hair blown by the winter winds.

"My heart ached for him," Charles Edison said. "He was no longer young, and everything was being destroyed. He then spotted me. And he said to me, 'Where is your mother? Find her. Bring her here. She will never see anything like this again as long as she lives!'"

The next morning, walking about the charred embers of so many of his hopes and dreams, the sixty-seven-year-old Edison mused, "There is great value in disaster. All our mistakes are burned up. Thank God! We can start all over again."

"Even though all these obstacles keep coming at you, you just have to keep going through them. Because it's worth it to do something in your life, as opposed to fantasizing about doing something."
—*Diane Keaton*

Follow His Lead

Humorist Will Rogers, having paid too much income tax one year, tried in vain to claim a rebate. His numerous letters and queries remained unanswered. Eventually the form for the next year's return arrived. In the section marked "DEDUCTIONS," Rogers listed: "Bad debt, US Government—$40,000."

Will Rogers on Growing Older

- ➤ Eventually you will reach a point when you stop lying about your age and start bragging about it.
- ➤ The older we get, the fewer things seem worth waiting in line for.
- ➤ Some people try to turn back their odometers. Not me. I want people to know "why" I look this way. I've traveled a long way and some of the roads weren't paved.
- ➤ When you are dissatisfied and would like to go back to youth, think of Algebra.
- ➤ You know you are getting old when everything either dries up or leaks.
- ➤ I don't know how I got over the hill without getting to the top.
- ➤ One of the many things no one tells you about aging is that it is such a nice change from being young.
- ➤ One must wait until evening to see how splendid the day has been.

> ➢ Being young is beautiful, but being old is comfortable.
> ➢ Long ago when men cursed and beat the ground with sticks, it was called witchcraft. Today it's called golf.
> ➢ And finally, if you don't learn to laugh at trouble, you won't have anything to laugh at when you are old.

"By the time a man is wise enough to watch his step, he's too old to go anywhere."
—*Billy Crystal*

A Nice New Place

Four girlfriends who had just graduated high school together made a pact to meet every ten years for dinner. They chose the Blue Gardenia Café for their first meal because some of the entrees were $20 for two and they didn't have much money and the waiters were really cute.

Ten years later, they again met at the Blue Gardenia because it had live music and a 2-for-1 happy hour.

The next three times they met at the Blue Gardenia because it had excellent lobsters, steaks and appetizers, an extensive wine list, and valet parking.

On their 50th reunion dinner, they decided to meet at the Blue Gardenia, because they'd never been there.

"I never think about age. I believe your age is totally how you feel. I've seen women of thirty-five who are old and people of seventy-five who are young. As long as I look after myself physically, mentally, and emotionally, I'll stay young."
—Joan Collins

Desiline Victor: Voting Legend

At age 102 and wheelchair bound, Desiline Victor sat in line for several hours waiting to vote at her Florida polling station on Election Day 2012. Her persistence and dedication to exercise her right to vote caught the attention of President Obama, who acknowledged her in his State of the Union address. Victor now has a bill named after her ("Desiline's Free and Fair Democracy Act") which will ease the voting process for everyone.

"Don't let aging get you down. It's too hard to get back up."
—*John Wagner*

Jiro Ono: Top Chef

Jiro Ono holds the Guinness World Record for oldest living chef. Many tout Ono, age eighty-seven, as the greatest sushi chef ever, and patrons clamber for seats at his Michelin three-star Tokyo restaurant, Sujiyabasji Jiro, where he still works. A festival favorite, the documentary *Jiro Dreams of Sushi* chronicles his life and work.

Ida Keeling: Record Breaker

In 2012, ninety-seven-year-old Ida Keeling set a record for the 100 Meter Sprint at the USA Track and Field Eastern Regional Open Championships. She finished the race at 51.85 seconds, beating the previous record of 59.9 seconds for the 90-and-over age category. Keeling took up running at age sixty-seven after several personal tragedies in her life, including the death of her husband and two of her sons.

"We'll be friends until we're old and senile. Then we'll be new friends."
—*Anonymous*

Senility Prayer

Grant me the senility to forget the people I never liked anyway, the good fortune to run into the ones I do, and the eyesight to tell the difference.

"When you're sixteen, you think twenty-eight is so old! And then you get to twenty-eight and it's fabulous. You think, then, what about forty-two? Ugh! And then forty-two is great. As you reach each age, you gain the understanding you need to deal with it and enjoy it."
—*Helen Mirren*

Have a Drink?

A very elderly gentleman, (mid nineties) very well dressed, hair well groomed, great looking suit, flower in his lapel smelling slightly of a good after-shave, presenting a well looked-after image, walks into an upscale cocktail lounge. Seated at the bar is an elderly lady, about mid-eighties.

The gentleman walks over, sits alongside of her, orders a drink, takes a sip, turns to her and says, "So tell me, do I come here often?"

Quite a Racket

Although he no longer has hair or his trademark James Bond stare, Sean Connery is still having tons of fun. A major tennis fan, Connery is featured here at the 2012 US Open where he personally congratulated fellow Brit Andy Murray.

Dabble This

George Weiss is eighty-four and he just may be the eldest mobile application inventor in America. His app is called Dabble—The Fast Thinking Word Game, and it is now available for iPhone, iPod touch, and iPad.

The object of the $0.99 game is to spell five words as quickly as possible using the twenty letters stacked in a pyramid shape. The five words must include a two, three, four, five and six letter word. The premise is simple and addictive. Dabble feels like the kind of old fashioned game you play with your grandparents— even grandparents reluctant to pick up an iPad.

"A lot has changed since 1958, but people still love a good game," Weiss said, reflecting on the year he first came up with the game.

"You know you're getting old when all the names in your black book had 'MD' after them."
—Harrison Ford

Finally Found It

John Milton completed his most famous work, *Paradise Lost*, in 1664, when he was fifty-six, composing the entire work over the course of six years while completely blind.

A Lot O'Rhyming

By the time of her death in 1886 aged fifty-five, Emily Dickinson had written nearly 1,800 poems. Only between seven and ten were published in her lifetime.

"Old age comes on suddenly, and not gradually as is thought."
—*Emily Dickinson*

"In old age we are like a batch of letters that someone has sent. We are no longer in the past, we have arrived."
—*Knut Hamsun,* Wanderers

Not Bored of the Rings

J. R. R. Tolkien wrote the first of his masterpiece Lord of the Rings trilogy in 1954, at the age of sixty-two.

Satchmo

Louis Armstrong was sixty-six years old when he became the oldest person to top the UK charts with "What a Wonderful World" in 1968.

Never too Old for the Slammer

In 1942 Mahatma Gandhi was imprisoned for two years in the Aga Khan palace, aged seventy-three, after drafting a non-violent resolution calling for the British to quit India.

Vindication

After a long imprisonment and famous release in 1994, Nelson Mandela became the first democratically elected President of South Africa at age seventy-six.

Nice Job

Clint Eastwood has won five Academy Awards, two of which are for best director. At age seventy-four in 2005, he was the oldest director to achieve this distinction for *Million Dollar Baby*.

Oldest Ever

At age eighty Jessica Tandy became the oldest person to win an Oscar, for Best Actress in *Driving Miss Daisy* in 1989.

Noble Nobel

Doris Lessing won the Nobel Prize for Literature in 2007 aged eighty-seven.

"After thirty, a body has a mind of its own."
—*Bette Midler*

Can't Stop Writing

Dame Barbara Cartland had written an estimated 723 novels by the time she died, at age ninety-eight in 2000.

Still Showing

Artist Louise Bourgeois reached the pinnacle of her career at age ninety-six, with a major retrospective at London's Tate Modern. She was also the first artist to fill Tate Modern's Turbine Hall when aged eighty-eight.

"I was blessed to look well and retain a youthful
look but that was just genes. I was disappointed
when critics started pointing out my wrinkles. I thought,
you mean this is what it's gonna be about now?
I'm not going to be permitted to be human?"
—Robert Redford

Starry Eyed

Charles Greeley Abbot, an American astrophysicist and astronomer aged 101 in 1973, was the oldest inventor ever to receive a patent. He died in the same year.

"Youth would be an ideal state if it came a little later in
life."
—Herbert Henry Asquith

Clear as a Bell

A man was telling his neighbor, "I just bought a new hearing aid. It cost me four thousand dollars, but it's state of the art. It's perfect."

"Really," answered the neighbor. "What kind is it?"

"Twelve thirty," he replied.

"When I look at myself as a younger actor, I see what a tight ass I was. I had a pretty big shadow because of my father and the comparisons. I was self-conscious about that. Now I realize there was nothing to be worried about."
—*Michael Douglas*

Oh Yeah?

Dave Farrow broke the *Guinness Book of World Records* by memorizing fifty-two decks worth of cards with focus and memorization techniques. Late in 2008, Dave broke his record by memorizing fifty-nine decks of cards. He had to learn to organize time, schedule time, and trigger focus—it was fourteen hours of straight memorizing for two days (with breaks for sleeping and eating). He was allowed to get some wrong, .05 percent. Out of the 3,068 cards he was allowed to get eighteen wrong, and he only missed one.

Follow the Rules

Hospital regulations require a wheelchair for patients being discharged. However, while working as a student nurse, I found one elderly gentleman already dressed and sitting on the bed with a suitcase at his feet who insisted he didn't need my help to leave the hospital. After a chat about rules being rules, he reluctantly let me wheel him to the elevator. On the way down I asked him if his wife was meeting him. "I don't know," he said. "She's still upstairs in the bathroom changing out of her hospital gown."

Old but Still Afloat

Debbie Reynolds was eighty-two when she published her tell-all biography, *Unsinkable*.

"True terror is to wake up one morning and discover that your high school class is running the country."
—*Kurt Vonnegut*

Still Talking

Although Jerry Stiller's career began in the 1960s, the eighty-six-year-old is still highly visible in contemporary Hollywood. Nearly everyone can recognize his trademark New York accent.

"The idea is that one's temperament improves with age; that you learn to deal better with people and become more benevolent and loving. That's not necessarily true. I try to stay loose but sometimes the best thing to do is get yourself away and take a good nap."
—Robert Duvall

But What About Finding a Job?

For many people, the "golden years" are a time to slow down and recall past achievements. Nola Ochs—a Guinness record holder as the world's oldest college graduate at age ninety-five—sees age as an opportunity to take on new challenges and satisfy unfulfilled goals. "I don't dwell on my age. It might limit what I can do. As long as I have my mind and health, age is just a number."

"Death is the number one killer in the world."
—*Anonymous*

*"Careers are here and they're gone. No matter how
great we think we are, we're nothing but the temples of*

Ozymandias—we're ruins in the making."
—William Shatner

Where's My Success?

Clara Peller had worked for thirty-five years as a manicurist at a local Chicago beauty salon. At age eighty, she was hired as a temporary manicurist for a television commercial set in a Chicago barbershop. Impressed by her no-nonsense manners and unique voice, the agency later asked her to sign a contract as an actress. Though hard of hearing and suffering from emphysema, which limited her ability to speak long lines of dialogue, Peller was quickly used in a number of TV spot advertisements, including a new commercial for the Wendy's Restaurant chain.

First airing on January 10, 1984, the Wendy's commercial portrayed a fictional fast-food competitor entitled "Big Bun," where three elderly ladies are served an enormous hamburger bun containing a minuscule hamburger patty. While two of the women are so engaged, they are interrupted by an irascible Peller, who searches in vain for customer assistance while making the outraged demand: "Where's the beef!"

Sequels featured a crotchety Peller yelling her famous line in various scenes, such as storming drive-thru counters, or in telephone calls to a fast-food executive attempting to relax on his yacht, the S.S. *Big Bun.*

Peller's "Where's the beef" line instantly became a catchphrase across the United States. The diminutive octogenarian actress made the three-word phrase a cultural phenomenon, and herself a cult star.

Papa or Grandpa?

"Piano Man" Billy Joel learned at age sixty-five that he was going to be a father for the second time. He'll be sixty-six when the new baby is born.

> *"You can't help getting older, but you don't have to get old."*
> —George Burns

Still Singing

The late Italian operatic tenor Luciano Pavarotti became a dad in 2003 when his wife gave birth to their youngest, a daughter named Alice. Pavarotti was fifty-eight at the time.

Worth the Wait

Laura Ingalls Wilder's best-selling series of books began with *Little House in the Big Woods*, which chronicled her pioneering childhood in the late 1800s. The books were so well-loved that NBC adapted one into a pilot and then the *Little House* television series, which aired from 1974 to 1982.

But Wilder didn't publish her first book until she was sixty-four. She started out as a teacher at the age of fifteen, and married Almanzo Wilder, a farmer, at eighteen. She wrote several articles on farming and rural life in the early 1900s, eventually becoming poultry editor for the *St. Louis Star*. Later in life, she started documenting her own story, at her daughter's encouragement. She finally published *Little House in the Big Woods* in 1932 and continued the series about herself and her family, ending with *These Happy Golden Years* in 1943, at age seventy-six.

What a Guy

Renaissance man Benjamin Franklin is known for many things—including founding the first public library in the US at age twenty-five, and establishing the first official fire department at twenty-nine. But he's also known for a much later achievement: signing the US Declaration of Independence. Franklin didn't put his John Hancock on that historic document until he was seventy, which made him the oldest signer.

"Wrinkles should merely indicate where smiles have been."
—*Mark Twain*

"When grace is joined with wrinkles, it is adorable. There is an unspeakable dawn in happy old age."
—*Victor Hugo*

One Step at a Time

Bill Wilson didn't start out as an activist or a counselor, but at age forty, he founded an organization that's helped millions of alcoholics regain control of their lives.

An army man and a businessman, Wilson struggled for most of his life with depression. After serving in the military during World War I, he went to Wall Street to work as a stock broker, where he was very successful despite being a heavy drinker. When the market crashed in 1929, Wilson's alcoholism spun out of control. In 1934, a friend who had overcome a drinking problem through principles found in the spiritual group, the Oxford Group, paid him a visit. Wilson didn't stop drinking immediately, but that conversation definitely made an impression. He entered a hospital to "dry out" and there had a religious experience that made him vow to stop drinking.

However, after leaving the hospital the Wilsons fell on tough financial times and he was desperate to have a drink again. He contacted another alcoholic, a surgeon named Robert Smith who also attended the Oxford Group. Their five-hour conversation kept Wilson from taking that drink. Realizing the value of one alcoholic helping another to keep from drinking, the two men searched for others to help.

In 1935, at age forty, Wilson teamed up with Dr. Smith to lay out the tenets of an organization devoted to helping alcoholics recover. But it wasn't until a 1941 *Saturday Evening Post* article that Alcoholics Anonymous really took off in popularity. Today, Alcoholics Anonymous is a worldwide organization that boasts more than two million members.

"Forty is the old age of youth; fifty the youth of old age."
—*Victor Hugo*

Hearing Is Fundamental

An elderly gentleman had serious hearing problems for a number of years.

He went to the doctor and the doctor was able to have him fitted for a set of hearing aids that allowed him to hear 100 percent.

He went back in a month and the doctor said, "Your hearing is perfect. Your family must be really pleased that you can hear again."

The gentleman replied, "Oh, I haven't told my family yet.

I just sit around and listen to the conversations. I've changed my will three times!"

Good Ideas
Gone Bad

The sudden energy and vitality that comes with thinking you are not only brilliant, but that your brilliance will soon bring fame and countless millions often is just that: Sudden. As in it won't last long because many of the jolts of inspiration are actually senior moments hidden in the confusion.

They Were Really Flying

In 1976, several airlines launched an ill-conceived marketing stunt and began giving away free drinks to coach passengers to convince people to fly. It became a very popular promotion, briefly. It soon became apparent that passengers weren't the only ones getting hammered: so were the companies' bottom lines, as passengers drank up their profits.

Just Say "No"

"The perfect beer for removing 'no' from your vocabulary for the night."

Budweiser's new Bud Light bottle? A special senior moment award to the guy who came up with the idea.

"The Bud Light Up for Whatever campaigns inspired millions of consumers to engage with our brand in a positive and light-hearted way," said one Bud vice president. "In this spirit, we created more than 140 different scroll messages intended to encourage brand engagement."

Well, yes it did. It inspired more than fourteen thousand people to sign a petition pointing out that the bottle and its message promotes "rape culture" over "consent culture."

Bud pulled the slogan.

Loving Sisters

Three sisters, ages ninety-two, ninety-four, and ninety-six, live in a house together. One night the ninety-six-year-old draws a bath. She puts her foot in and pauses.

She yells to the other sisters, "Was I getting in or out of the bath?"

The ninety-four-year-old yells back, "I don't know. I'll come up and see."

She starts up the stairs and pauses. "Was I going up the stairs or down?"

CHAPTER NINE | 179

> The ninety-two-year-old is sitting at the kitchen table having tea, listening to her sisters. She shakes her head and says, "I sure hope I never get that forgetful, knock on wood."
>
> She then yells, "I'll come up and help both of you as soon as I see who's at the door."

Maybe Try Again in February

Snapple attempted to erect the world's largest popsicle in 2005 in Times Square. It was made of frozen Snapple juice, twenty-five feet tall, and weighed 17.5 tons. But the company didn't count on the 80-degree weather and the frozen tower melted, sending kiwi-strawberry-flavored fluid pouring onto the streets of downtown Manhattan.

Not So Magic

Jim McCafferty, a magician turned marketer, was trying to promote his marketing startup business in 1990 by allowing himself to be put in a straight-jacket and then enclosed in a welded-shut steel cage and hoisted by a crane to a height of 300 feet. But during the stunt, the cage malfunctioned before he could attach himself to a harness. Time ran out, and the cage plunged sixty feet before he clicked himself into the harness, just seconds before the cage smashed into the ground. He was taken to the hospital suffering from first- and second-degree rope burns.

Streak of Bad Luck

At a 2002 rugby match between archrivals New Zealand and Australia, two streakers interrupted the game, wearing nothing but the Vodafone logo. Police arrested the streakers before the match was over, and one of the CEOs of Vodafone was forced to apologize afterwards for encouraging these two guys to streak through the game—and thus break the law. The company also ended up donating $30,000 to a nonprofit campaign aimed at reducing sports injuries.

No Cred

In 2002, Sony had graffiti artists design—and spray paint—various pictures of their PlayStation Portable at several locations around New York City. But many people hated the look of the ads, and others saw it as a blatant attempt to be cool, or to get cheap labor from struggling teenagers. An online petition was started with comments like, "Stop cynically exploiting graffiti artists." Another declared, "I will never buy a Sony product again."

The Talent-less Beatles

Years before The Beatles launched their international fame on the *Ed Sullivan Show* in 1964, they were rejected by the same show.

Mike Smith and Dick Rowe were executives in charge of evaluating new talent for the London office of Decca Records. On December 13, 1961, Mike Smith traveled to Liverpool to watch a local rock 'n' roll band perform. He decided they had talent, and invited them to audition on New Year's Day 1962. The group made the trip to London and spent two hours playing fifteen different songs at the Decca studios. Then they went home and waited for an answer. They waited for weeks. Finally, Rowe told the band's manager that the label wasn't interested because they sounded too much like a popular group called The Shadows. In one of the most famous of all rejection lines, he said: "Not to mince words, Mr. Epstein, but we don't like your boys' sound. Groups are out; four-piece groups with guitars particularly are finished."

Who'll Watch?

John and Forrest Mars, the owners of Mars Incorporated, the makers of M&M's, were invited by Universal Studios and asked for permission to use M&M's in a new film they were making. The Mars brothers said "no." The film was *E.T. The Extra-Terrestrial* directed by Steven Spielberg. The M&M's were needed for a crucial scene: Eliott, the little boy who befriended the alien, uses candies to lure E.T. into his house. Instead, Universal Studios went to Hershey's and cut a deal to use a new product called Reese's Pieces. Initial sales of Reese's Pieces had been light. But when *E.T.* became a top-grossing film—generating tremendous publicity for "E.T.'s favorite candy"—sales exploded, tripling within two weeks and continuing to climb for months. "It was the biggest marketing coup in history," one Hershey executive said. "We got immediate recognition for our product. We would normally have to pay 15 or 20 million bucks for it."

"What I've learned in this first fifty is that if you can allow yourself to breathe into the depth, wonder, beauty, craziness, and strife—everything that represents the fullness of your life—you can live fearlessly. Because you come to realize that if you just keep breathing, you cannot be conquered."
—*Oprah Winfrey*

They Sparkled, The Idea Fizzled

A candy company in Berlin in the 1920s tried dropping foil-wrapped chocolates on its citizens to advertise their services. But police had to step in after they received complaints of injuries from the falling sweets.

Quick Cash

No one at Fox expected much from the television show *M*A*S*H* when it debuted 1972. Executives simply wanted to make a cheap series by using the *M*A*S*H* movie set again—so it was a surprise when it became Fox's only hit show. Three years later, the company was hard up for cash. When the *M*A*S*H* ratings started to slip after two of its stars left, Fox executives panicked and sold syndication rights to the first seven seasons of *M*A*S*H*. Enough local stations took the deal so that Fox made $25 million. They celebrated. But briefly it seems. When *M*A*S*H* finally aired in syndication in 1979, it became one of the most successful syndicated shows ever, second only to *I Love Lucy*. Each of the original 168 episodes grossed over $1 million for local TV stations; Fox got nothing.

> *"Youth is wasted on the young."*
> —*Oscar Wilde or George Bernard Shaw*

> *"Adults are obsolete children."*
> —*Dr. Seuss*

George and Sheila

There were two elderly people, George and Sheila, living in a North Carolina mobile home park. He was a widower and she a widow and they had known one another for a number of years.

One evening a supper was held in the communal refectory and the two found themselves at the same table, seated across from one another. As the meal progressed, George made several admiring glances at Sheila and he finally gathered his courage to ask her, "Sheila, will you marry me?"

After about five seconds of careful consideration, Sheila answered. "Yes. Yes, I will."

The meal ended and, with a few more pleasant exchanges, they went to their respective trailers. Next morning, George was troubled: "Did she say yes or did she say no?" He couldn't remember. Not even a faint memory. So it was with some trepidation that he went to the telephone and called Sheila. First, he explained that he didn't remember as well as he used to. Then he reviewed the lovely evening past. As he gained a little more courage, George inquired gingerly, "Sheila, when I asked if you would marry me, did you say yes or did you say no?"

George was delighted to hear Sheila say, "Why, I said, yes, yes I will, and I meant it with all my heart." Then she continued, "I am so glad that you called, because I couldn't remember for the life of me who had asked."

"It isn't so astonishing, the number of things that I can remember, as the number of things I can remember that aren't so."
—Mark Twain

So They'll Visit

An elderly woman decided to prepare her will and told her preacher she had two final requests. First, she wanted to be cremated, and second, she wanted her ashes scattered over Wal-Mart. "Wal-Mart?" the preacher exclaimed. "Why Wal-Mart?" "Then I'll be sure my daughters visit me twice a week."

"The best classroom in the world is at the feet of an elderly person."
—Andy Rooney

The Electrical Toy?

William Orton was president of the Western Union Telegraph Company in 1876. Western Union had a monopoly on the telegraph, the world's most advanced communications technology, which made it one of America's richest and most powerful companies, "with $41 million in capital and the pocketbooks of the financial world behind it." So when Gardiner Greene Hubbard, a wealthy Bostonian, approached Orton with an offer to sell the patent for a new invention Hubbard had helped to fund, Orton treated it as a joke. Hubbard was asking for $100,000. Orton bypassed Hubbard and drafted a response directly to the inventor.

"Mr. Bell," he wrote, "after careful consideration of your invention, while it is a very interesting novelty, we have come to the conclusion that it has no commercial possibilities . . . What use could this company make of an electrical toy?" The invention, the telephone, would have been perfect for Western Union. The company had a nationwide network of telegraph wires in place, and the inventor, twenty-nine-year-old Alexander Graham Bell, had shown that his telephone worked quite well on telegraph lines. All the company had to do was hook telephones up to its existing lines and it would have had the world's first nationwide telephone network in a matter of months. Instead, Bell kept the patent and in a few decades his telephone company, "renamed American Telephone and Telegraph (AT&T), had become the largest corporation in America. The Bell patent— offered to Orton for a measly $100,000—became the single most valuable patent in history."

"I'm always trying to tackle subjects that tax me and make me think. That's the key to staying young at heart. The brain has to be exercised the same as the rest of the body."
—Clint Eastwood

We Can Crush Them with This

Schlitz Brewing Company was America's number-two beer in 1970, behind Budweiser.

A company executive discovered what he thought was a way to change that. He figured that if he could cut the cost of ingredients used in his beer and speed up the brewing process at the same time, he could brew more beer in the same amount of time for less money, and earn higher profits.

He cut the amount of time it took to brew Schlitz from forty days to fifteen, and replaced much of the barley malt in the beer with corn syrup, which was cheaper. He also switched from one type of foam stabilizer to another to get around new labeling laws that would have required the original stabilizer to be disclosed on the label. He got what he wanted: a cheaper, more profitable beer that made a lot of money—at first. But it tasted terrible, and tended to break down so quickly that the cheap ingredients bonded together and sank to the bottom of the can, forming a substance that "looked disconcertingly like mucus."

Suddenly Schlitz found itself shipping out a great deal of apparently snot-ridden beer. The brewery knew about it pretty quickly and made a command decision to do nothing. Sales plummeted and Schlitz began a long steady slide from the top three. Schlitz finally caved in and recalled 10 million cans of the snot beer. But their reputation was ruined and sales never recovered. In 1981, they shut down their Milwaukee brewing plant; the following year the company was purchased by rival Stroh's. One former mayor of Milwaukee compared the brewery's fortunes to the sinking of the Titanic, asking "How could that big of a business go under so fast?"

Model T Is Forever!

When Henry Ford first marketed the Model T in 1908, it was a state-of-the-art automobile. Over the years, the price went down dramatically and as the first truly affordable quality automobile, the Model T revolutionized American culture. The Model T was the only car that the Ford Motor Company made. As the auto industry grew and competition got stiffer, everyone in the company—from Ford's employees to his family—pushed him to update the design.

In 1912, Ford took his family on their first visit to Europe. When he returned he discovered that his top aides had prepared a surprise for him: a new, low-slung version of the Model T, and the prototype stood in the middle of the factory floor, its gleaming red lacquerwork polished to a high sheen.

The first thing Ford did when he saw the car was rip off one of its front doors. The he proceeded to destroy the whole car with his bare hands. It was a message to everyone around him not to mess with his prize creation.

Apparently he did not like anyone tampering with his prize.

Thus, by 1925, after more than fifteen years on the market, the Model T was pretty much the same car it had been when it debuted. While Ford rested on his laurels for a decade and a half, his competitors continued to innovate. Automobile buyers took notice and began trading up. By the time Ford finally announced that a replacement for the Model T was in the works in May 1927, the company had already lost the battle. That year, Chevrolet sold more cars than Ford for the first time. And from 1930 on, Ford Motor Company had to be content with second place.

"Anyone who stops learning is old, whether at twenty or eighty. Anyone who keeps learning stays young. The greatest thing in life is to keep your mind young."
—*Henry Ford*

It Glows, and So Will You

In 1889, Marie Curie and husband Pierre discovered radium and coined the term radioactive. And while little was known about the alkaline earth metal, one thing was for sure: it glowed in the dark. Suddenly, the public was captivated by radium's luminescence. Manufacturers painted airplane dials, instruments, and watch faces with radium, spawning a huge glow-in-the-dark fad. Women began painting their nails with it to impress suitors, for Halloween, people even coated their faces with the stuff to get that oh-so-ghoulish look.

A dentist in New Jersey noticed that many of his patients who worked at US Radium suffered from deteriorating jaws or phossy jaw. Worse still, the Essex County coroner discovered that women from a radium plant were dying of severe anemia and leukemia. By 1925, he'd collected enough data to prove that radiation was so high in the women's bodies that it was likely the cause of death. As if exposure to the material wasn't bad enough, many of the watch-painting women had been dipping the tip of their paintbrushes in their mouths to make a finer point for painting tiny numbers on watches. Unfortunately, it took physicians a little while to officially link the substance with cancer.

The Face in the Mirror

I was sitting in the waiting room for my first appointment with a new dentist when I noticed his diploma, which had his full name.

Suddenly, I remembered a tall, handsome dark-haired boy with the same name I had gone to high school with more than forty years before.

I wondered, could he be the same guy I had a crush on so many years before?

After seeing him, I quickly ended the thought. The guy I was looking at had a deeply lined face and was way too old to have been my classmate.

After he examined my teeth, I asked him if he had attended Strong Vincent High School.

"Yes, I did," he said. "I'm a Scorpion."

"When did you graduate?" I asked.

"In 1975. Why?"

"You were in my class!" I exclaimed.

He looked at me closely.

"What did you teach?" he asked, ruining what had been a perfect day.

Question: What do a coffin and a condom have in common?

Answer: They're both filled with stiffs—except one's coming and one's going.

Ross?

In 1979, Ross Perot employed some of his well-known business acumen and foresaw that Bill Gates was on his way to building Microsoft into a great company. So he offered to buy him out. Gates says Perot offered between $6 million and $15 million; Perot says that Gates wanted $40 million to $60 million. Whatever the numbers were, the two couldn't come to terms, and Perot walked away empty-handed. Today, Microsoft is worth hundreds of billions of dollars.

Follow the Money

In 1979, the *Washington Post* offered the *San Francisco Chronicle* the opportunity to syndicate a series of articles that two reporters named Bob Woodward and Carl Bernstein were writing about a break-in at the Democratic headquarters at Washington, D.C.'s Watergate Hotel. Owner Charles Thieriot said no. "There will be no West Coast interest in the story," he explained. Thus, his rival, the *San Francisco Examiner,* was able to purchase the rights to the hottest news story of the decade for $500.

Remember Them?

Way back when, the W. T. Grant variety store chain was one of the nation's largest retailers. At one point it decided that the best way to increase sales was to increase the number of customers—by offering credit and putting tremendous pressure on store managers to issue credit. Employees who didn't meet their credit quotas risked complete humiliation. They had pies thrown in their faces, were forced to push peanuts across the floor with their noses, and were sent through hotel lobbies wearing only diapers. Eager to avoid such total embarrassment, store managers gave credit "to anyone who breathed," including untold thousands of customers who were bad risks. W. T. Grant racked up $800 million worth of bad debts before it finally collapsed in 1977.

"I don't think we get smarter as we get older, we just run out of stupid things to do."
—*Anonymous*

What Does He Know?

IBM once hired Microsoft founder Bill Gates to come up with the operating software for a new computer that IBM was rushing to market, and Gates turned to a company called Digital Research. He set up a meeting between Digital's owner and IBM. The owner couldn't make the meeting and sent his wife instead. She turned down a contract offer from IBM. Bill Gates went elsewhere, eventually coming up with a program called DOS, the software that put Microsoft on the map.

"Two things are infinite: the universe and human stupidity; and I'm not sure about the universe."
—*Albert Einstein*

Just One Drawback: Death

In the early 1900s, designers offered the perfect solution for women who hated seeing a dirty ashtray on the kitchen table—asbestos tablecloths. In fact, housewives (and magicians) were delighted to find out that asbestos materials came with a neat cleaning trick: if you set an asbestos tablecloth on fire, stains would come out, and the things would look brand new. No more washing and drying. Of course, with such a novel, fireproof material in their hands, suppliers didn't want to limit asbestos' potential to the kitchen table. So, they expanded to kitchen clothing. "Careless ladies" who leaned against the stove and caught fire didn't have to worry anymore thanks to asbestos aprons and oven mitts. Although humans had used asbestos since the Greek and Roman empires (and even though physicians back then noticed that exposure to the fibrous material caused lung ailments), the United States didn't start investigating asbestos' negative affects until the 1970s. While it took governments centuries to ban asbestos, lawyers caught on much faster and meso-thelioma attorneys have been suing companies ever since.

"Happiness is nothing more than good health and a bad memory."
—*Albert Schweitzer*

"There's never enough time to do all the nothing you want."
—*Bill Watterson,* The Authoritative Calvin and Hobbes

Anything for Clean Teeth

It's tough reaching those back molars with dental floss, and it's tough reaching those back molars to floss them. That's why Oral-B created the Hummingbird flosser, the Cadillac of dental aids. The ergonomically designed, vibrating electric flosser was made to gently massage those hard to reach spots and turn the flossing experience into a dream. Oral-B investors had no idea the Hummingbird flosser would make picking padlocks a dream, too. With a few modifications—mainly changing the power source from an AAA battery to a D battery and replacing the floss with a pick just about anyone could create a vibrating pick that will pop open most padlocks. Even those inept at building can follow the step-by-step directions on the Web.

"Don't worry about avoiding temptation . . . as you grow older, it will avoid you."
—Winston Churchill

"Maybe it's true that life begins at fifty . . . but everything else starts to wear out, fall out, or spread out."
—Phyllis Diller

Payback

Childhood: That time of life when you make funny faces in the mirror.
Middle Age: That time of life when the mirror gets even.

"Aging is not lost youth, but a new stage of opportunity and strength."
—Betty Friedan

Where Eagles Dare

To the cheers of bird lovers everywhere, conservationists reintroduced white-tailed sea eagles to East Scotland, where they haven't lived for two hundred years. As a safeguard for the raptors, they were placed on the protected-species list.

These protected birds now have free rein to attack livestock and civilians alike—an activity they seem very much to enjoy and, apparently, are quite good at.

Quotes on Retirement

Retirement is wonderful. It's doing nothing without worrying about getting caught at it.
— Gene Perret

The two most dangerous years of your life are the year you are born and the year you retire.
— Liz Davidson

The money's no better in retirement but the hours are!
—Terri Guillemets

Retirement kills more people than hard work ever did.
—Malcolm Forbes

Sometimes it's hard to tell if retirement is a reward for a lifetime of hard work or a punishment.
—Terri Guillemets

Retire from work, but not from life.
—M.K. Soni

Don't simply retire from something; have something to retire to.
—Harry Emerson Fosdick

I'm not just retiring from the company, I'm also retiring from my stress, my commute, my alarm clock, and my iron.
—Hartman Jule

The trouble with retirement is that you never get a day off.
—Abe Lemons

A retired husband is often a wife's full-time job.
—Ella Harris

Retirement is having nothing to do and someone always keeping you from it.
—Robert Brault

"If I had my life to live over I'd like to make more mistakes next time. I'd relax. I would limber up. I would be sillier than I have been this trip. I would take fewer things seriously. I would take more chances. I would climb more mountains and swim more rivers. I would eat more ice cream and less beans. I would perhaps have more actual trouble, but I'd have fewer imaginary ones. You see, I'm one of those people who live sensibly and sanely hour after hour, day after day. Oh, I've had my moments, and if I had to do it over again, I'd have more of them. In fact, I'd try to have nothing else. Just moments, one after another, instead of living so many years ahead of each day. I've been one of those persons who never goes anywhere without a thermometer, a hot water bottle, a

raincoat, and a parachute. If I had to do it again, I would travel lighter that I have. If I had my life to live over, I would start barefoot earlier in the spring and stay that way later in the fall. I would go to more dances. I would ride more merry-go-rounds, I would pick more daisies."
—*Nadine Stair*

Conclusion

"To be able to forget means sanity."
—*Jack London,* The Star Rover

"Without forgetting it is quite impossible to live at all."
—*Friedrich Nietzsche*

I'm on board with Jack and Fred. Forgetting is actually a good thing—a benefit to a life well lived, the key to enjoying every moment, or at least those you remember.

So I'm fuzzy on a number of things, and others I cannot recall at all. So what? I often just pretend to remember stuff as a way of humoring my friends as we stroll down Memory Lane. Remember that time in junior year when you streaked naked down College Avenue? No, I don't. But I'll say I do. It makes the afternoon go faster to just go along with it.

One thing I can still remember is an old schoolyard rejoinder that went—cleaned up here for general audiences—"I've forgotten more about (*insert activity here*) than you even knew." That's how I view the process of forgetting. If we are older, we've all taken in vast amounts of facts along the way, oceans of information. Dropping some of that stuff into the abyss we call forgetfulness is not bad. It shows we've learned too much.

I will take one thing from the effort of writing this book. I enjoyed it, pure and simple. I was energized by the exercise. I can only hope that you remember how to read so you can enjoy it as well, though I suppose there are some advantages to having someone read it to you.

We should all take the phenomenon of forgetting to heart. We have all reached the point where we are entitled to forget things. Ours cups runneth over. The one single thing I would say I've learned from putting this book together is to keep moving, keep trying, keep doing.

Take for example a woman named Nola Ochs. While many people in their dotage slow down and look back, Nola Ochs became the world's oldest college graduate at age ninety-five, which earned her a spot in the *Guinness Book of World Records*. When somebody asked Nola why she had bothered with it at all, she said, "I don't dwell on my age. It might limit what I can do. Age is just a number."

Well played there, Nola.

We can all take something away from that.

Or take Clint Eastwood, who's a long way from his *The Good, the Bad, and the Ugly* days and still kicking hard as he heads into his mid-eighties. "I'm always trying to tackle subjects that tax me and make me think. That's the key to staying young at heart. The brain has to be exercised the same as the rest of the body."

The fact is that the most important thing, the most energizing thing, is to keep kicking, and keep kicking hard. The minute you think it's time to sit back and relax, you will become a potted plant on the window sill, hoping someone will come along and water you.

Live with no regrets and keep moving—a rolling stone gathers no moss and all that hooey. Live like someone just left the gate open.

Here is what prolific and highly regarded science fiction author Isaac Asimov said when asked what he would do if he were told he had only one day more to live:

"Type faster."

Which reminds me of a good one:

The doctor looks up at his patient over his clipboard, holding a lab report.

"I have some bad news, and some very bad news," he said.

The startled patient jumps at a bit and says, "Well, I guess you should give me the bad news first."

"The lab called with your results," the doctor says. "They said you have twenty-four hours to live."

"Twenty-four hours! Good lord that's terrible news. What in God's name could be worse than that? What's the very bad news?"

"I've been trying to reach you since yesterday"

While you're forgetting, try to make a difference. Be grateful you've lasted this long. Help someone. As the late and wise curmudgeon Andy Rooney once said, "The best classroom in the world is at the feet of an elderly person."

Here's something I often take to heart:
An old man was walking on the beach one morning after a storm. In the distance he could see someone moving like a dancer. As he came closer, he saw it was a young woman picking up starfish and throwing them back into the sea.

"Young lady," he asked, "why are you throwing starfish into the ocean?"

"She looked at him quizzically and said, "The sun is up and the tide I going out, and if I do not thrown them back into the water they will die."

"But young lady," he replied, "do you not realize there are many miles of beach and thousands of starfish? You cannot possibly make a difference."

The young woman listened politely, then bent down, picked up another starfish, and gently tossed it back into the rolling and welcoming waves.

"It made a difference for that one."

Now put this book down and go make a difference.

"Setting a good example of your children takes all the fun out of middle age."
—*William Feather*

INDEX

A Day at the Races 115

Abbot, Charles Greeley 164

Abbott, Greg 132

Abdul-Jabbar, Kareem 77

Adams, John 130

Adams, Franklin P. 72, 88

Adams, Scott 122

Aguilera, Christina 30–31

Alcoholics Anonymous 172–174

Allen, Ethan 125

American Idol 29

Armstrong, Louis 161

Askri, Khalid 58

Asquith, Herbert Henry 164

Astaire, Fred 41

AT&T 186–187

Authoritative Calvin and Hobbes, The 95

Bacon, Francis 113

Ball, Lucille 10

Balboa, Rocky 20

Bank of America 6–7

Barber, Jerry 72

Beatles, The 181–182

Beckles, Albert 72

Beethoven, Ludwig van 44

Belichick, Bill 76

Bell, Alexander Graham 186–188

Bennett, Dan 88

Bergen, Candace 149

Bernstein, Carl 194

Berra, Yogi 51, 53, 122

Biden, Joe 137–138, 139, 141

Bierce, Ambrose 123, 147

Bing, Dave 135

Blanc, Mel 120

Blanchard, Mike "Flathead" 118

Blanda, George 69–71

Bolt, Usain 104

Bonaparte, Napoleon 64

Bond, James (film character) 158

Bonney, William H. (Billy the Kid) 125

Book of Life, The 46–47

"Born to Be Wild" x

Boston Red Sox 67–68, 74–75

Bourgeois Louis 164

Boys Don't Cry 37

Bradshaw, Terry 63

Brault, Robert 202

Brockovich, Erin 44–45

Brownworth, Merri 12

Bud Light 177–178

Budweiser 177–178, 188–189

Burns, George 5, 83, 98, 148, 170

Bush, George W. xvii, 130, 140, 141, 142–144

Cano, Robinson 54

Canseco, Jose 60–61

Capone, Alphonse "Al" 125

Caray, Harry 63

Carbo, Bernie 74–75

Carlin, George 119

Carnegie, Andrew 120, 128

Carney, Jay 139, 145

Carpenter, Karen 117

Carter, Jimmy xvi, 25, 142

Cartland, Barbara 163

Chicago White Sox 62–63

Christie, Agatha 39–40

Churchill, Winston 118, 198

Citizen Kane 134

Clemenceau, Georges 88

Cleveland Browns 70

Cleveland Indians 63–64

Cleveland Stadium 60

Clinton, Hillary 141

Clough, Brian 110

Collins, Joan 154

Comiskey Park 62–63

Confucius 101

Connery, Sean 158

Copa Libertadores (soccer) 58

Crabbe, Buster xiv

Cruz, Jose 52

Crystal, Billy 153

Curie, Pierre 191–192

Curie, Marie 191–192

Dahl, DJ Steve 62–63

Dallas Cowboys 71

Dangerfield, Rodney 86, 121

Darrow, Clarence 115

Darwin, Charles 41

David, Jefferson 123

Davis, Fred 72

Davis Jr., Sammy 124

Davis, Al 70

Davis, Bette 127

Davis, Marvin 22

Davidson, Liz 200

Day, Doris 90

Decca Records 181–182

Denver Broncos 70

Detroit Tigers 66, 74–75

Dickinson, Emily 160, 161

Digital Research 195

Diller, Phyllis 198

Douglas, Michael 165

Driving Miss Daisy 162

Dunbar, Quinton 59–60

Duva, Lou 68

Duvall, Robert 167

E. T.: The Extra-Terrestrial 182–183

Earp, Wyatt 124

Eastwood, Clint 162, 188, 207

Ed Sullivan Show 181–182

Edison, Charles 150–151

Edison, Thomas 42, 150–151

Einstein, Albert xvii, 9, 20, 33, 38, 196

Ellis, Dock 76

Erin Brockovich 44–45

Ertz, Susan 93

FAR Rabat (soccer club) 58

Farrow, Dave 165–166

Ferrell, Will 35

Feather, William 113, 209

Finding Nemo 46–47

Finley, Charles 67–68

Fisher, Dorothy Canfield 85

Fitzgerald, F. Scott 121

Forbes, Malcolm 201

Ford, Harrison 160

Fosdick, Harry Emerson 201

Ford Motor Co. 189–191

Ford, Henry 189–191

Ford, Rob 135–136

Foreman, George 73

Fox (television) 183–184

Frank, Scott 117

Franklin, Benjamin 39, 125, 172

French Foreign Legion xiv

Frerotte, Gus 55–56

Friedan, Betty 198

Frost, Robert 121, 135

Gambon, Michael 31

Gandhi, Mahatma 161–162

Gates, Bill 193, 195
Georgia Southern University 59–60
Gibbs, Robert 138
"Girls Just Wanna Have Fun" 30
Goldwyn, Samuel 122
Good, the Bad, and the Ugly, The 207
Google xvi
Grant, W. T. 194–195
Great Gatsby, The 121
Green Bay Packers 30–31
Green, Dallas 61
Griffin, Merv 120
Guillemets, Terri 200, 201
*Guinness Book of World
    Records* 165–166

Halapio, Jon 59–60
Hall, Skip 72
Halliwell, Geri 45
Hallmark 147
Hamsun, Knut 161
Hancock, John 172
Harper, Valerie 149
Harris, Kalama 138–139
Harrison, Jonotthan 59–60
Harris, Ella 202
Harry Potter (films) 31
Hart, Gary 140–141
Hayes, Helen 89
Hefner, Hugh 47
Helms, Buddy 72
Hemingway, Ernest 124
Henderson, Thomas
    "Hollywood" 71
"Here Comes the Bride" 35
Hershey 182–183
Hitchcock, Alfred 118
Holliday, Doc 118
Holyfield, Evander 57, 75–76

Hoover, Herbert 27–28
Hope, Bob 12, 87, 88
Hostetler, Jeff 55–56
Houston Astros 51–52, 53–54
Howe, Gordie 72
Hubbard, Gardiner Greene 186–187
Hugo, Victor 172, 174

I Love Lucy 184
IBM 195
Indian Proverb 124

Jade Helm 15 132–133
Jackson, Holbrook 22
James, Jesse 125
Jaworski, Ron 72
Jiro Dreams of Sushi 155
Joel, Billy 165
Johnson, Samuel 103
Jolie, Angelina 35
Jordan, Michael 52
Jule, Hartman 201
Jumping the Queue 147

Kansas City Chiefs 70
Keaton, Diane 10, 151
Keats, John 121
Keeling, Ida 156
Keillor, Garrison 123
Kerry, John 140, 145
Kiner, Ralph 61
King, Larry 56
Kipling, Rudyard 120
Knight, Bobby 51
Koufax, Sandy 52
Kyodo News 103

Lamonica, Daryle 70
Lemons, Abe 201

Lasorda, Tommy 65

Lauper, Cyndi 30

Lessing, Doris 162

Lewis, C. S. 27

Little House in the Big Woods 171

Little House on the Prarie 171

Lohan, Lindsay 28–29

Long, Russell 130–132

Los Angeles Dodgers 65, 66–67

"Louie Louie" ix

Love in a Time of Cholera 113

Lowe, Chad 37

M&M's 182–183

*M*A*S*H* 182–183

Madden, John 79

Madison Square Garden 140

Mamby, Saoul 72

Mandela, Nelson 162

Mantle, Mickey 60

Marciano, Rocky 52

Marquez, Gabriel
    Garcia 113

Mars Incorporated 182–183

Marx, Groucho 90, 115

Mayer, Louis B. 122

Meir, Golda 136

McCafferty, Jim 179–180

McCain, John 136, 137, 145

McCreery, Scotty 29

McQ 18

Mencken, H. L. 65, 107, 147

Menino, Thomas M. 134–135

Merkel, Angela 141

Miami Herald 140

Microsoft 193, 195

Midler, Bette 100, 163

Mighty Joe Young 75

Milligan, Spike 118

Million Dollar Baby 37, 162

Milton, John 160

Mirren, Helen 157

Mitlancer 99

Miyazaki, Hidekichi 104

Mondesi, Raul 65

Monkey Business (ship) 140–141

Montana, Joe 79

Monterrey (soccer club) 58

Moreau, Jeanne 81

Murray, Andy 158

Nash, Ogden xii, 87

National Enquirer 140

Navratilova, Martina 78–79

New York Daily News 144

New York Giants 55

New York Jets 54

New York Mets 61

New York Times 134–135

New York Yankees 54, 75

Newton, Issac 31, 42, 47

Nicholson, Jack 29

Niekro, Joe 52

Nietzsche, Friedrich 72, 205

Norman, Greg 59

Norris, Chuck 133–134

Oakland Athletics 68

Oakland Raiders 70

Obama, Barack 133–134, 136, 137–138,
    139, 141, 155

Obamacare 139

Ochs, Nola 167–168

O'Neal, Shaquille 51

Oral-B 197–198

Orton, William 186–187

Overbay, Lyle 54

Ozark, Danny 64

Pagnozzi, Matt 54
Paige, Satchel 15, 66, 67–68, 72, 91
Paradise Lost 160
Patton, Solomon 59–60
Pavarotti, Luciano 170–171
Pease, Brent 60
Peduto, Bill 21
Pellman, Don 109–110
Perot, Ross 193
Perry, Rick 128–129
Perret, Gene 200
Phelps, Michael 74
Piersall, Jimmy 61
Pitt, Brad 35
Pittsburgh Pirates 76
Pittsburgh Steelers 30–31, 70
Poe, Edgar Allan 122
Pope John XXIII 106
Pope Paul VI 113
Popeye 112
Pratchett, Terry 25
Quan, Jean 127–128

Raddle, Donald 88
Reagan, Ronald 87, 130–131
Redford, Robert 164
Reese's Pieces 182
Reynolds, Debbie 166
Roberts, Julia 44
Robinson, Jackie 77
Rodriguez, Chi Chi 52
Rogers, Will 19, 151–152, 152–153
Ronaldinho 58
Rooney, Andy 84–85, 186
Roosevelt, Eleanor 133
Roosevelt, Theodore 133
Rough Riders 38
Rowe, Dick 181

S.S. *Big Bun* 170
Saldana, Zoe 46–47

Salisbury, Ed 122
San Diego Chargers 70, 76
San Diego Padres 76
San Francisco 49ers 76
San Francisco Chronicle 194
San Francisco Examiner 194
Sanchez, Mark 54
Sanders, Barry 52
Sanders, Harland (Colonel Sanders) 148
Santana, Carlos ix, x
Santayana, George x
Sarandon, Susan 30
Saturday Evening Post 174
Schlitz Brewing Company 188–189
Schopenhauer, Arthur 113
Schweitzer, Albert 197
Sendak, Maurice 10
Seuss, Dr. 184
Shadows, The 182
Shatner, William 169
Sinatra, Frank 124
Singh, Faukja 108
Singh, Raja Maharaj 72
Skinner, Todd 123
Smith, Mike 181
Smith, Robert 172–174
Smith, Roscoe 57
Soni, M. K. 201
Sony 180–181
Sony (Playstation) 180–181
Sophocles 16
Spice Girls 45
Spielberg, Steven 182
Sporting News, The 71
St. Louis Cardinals 65
St. Louis Star 171
Stair, Nadine 202–203
Stallone, Sylvester 20
Stanley, Edward (Earl of Derby) 104
"Star-Spangled Banner" 30
Stein, Gertrude 41

Stengel, Casey 8, 53
Steppenwolf x
Stiller, Jerry 167
Stockdale, Admiral James 130
Stoppard, Tom 113
Swank, Hilary 37

Tandy, Jessica 162
Texas Rangers 60, 63–64
These Happy Golden Years 171
Thomas, Helen 117
Thoreau, Henry David 105
Tolkien, J. R. R. xiv, 161
Tomlin, Lily 2
Trinity College 41
Twain, Mark xvii, 42, 103, 108, 122, 124, 172, 185

Universal Studios 182
University of Florida 59–60
University of Michigan 89–90
University of South Carolina 74
University of Texas 57
Unsinkable 166

Veeck, Bill 62–63
Voice, The 30–31
Vonnegut, Kurt 166
Wagner, John 155
Wal-Mart 186
Wanderers 161
Watterson, Bill 197
Washington Post 194
Washington Redskins 55–56, 71
Watergate 64
Weiner, Anthony 96–97
Wesley, Mary 147
Western Michigan Whitecaps 66
Western Union Telegraph Company 186–187

Westheimer, Dr. Ruth 85–86
"What a Wonderful World" 161
Wheeler, Major General Joseph 37–38
White, Betty 33, 105
Whittier, John Greenleaf 42
Wilde, Oscar 184
Wilder, Almanzo 171
Wilder, Laura Ingalls xiv, 171
Wilson, Bill 172–174
Winfrey, Oprah 183
WLUP (radio station) 62
Wonder, Stevie 36
Woodstock (concert) x
Woodward, Bob 194
Woolf, Virginia 36
Wright, Stephen 27

Yastrzemski, Carl 68
Yeats, W. B. 41

Zapatero, Jose Luis Rodriguez 137